Leading Your POSItively Outrageous Service Team

T. Scott Gross

You probably know him as the creator of Positively Outrageous Service, but at home he's known as Dad, Tiger and even occasionally Scookiebuttons. Whatever you call him, T. Scott Gross is known for the gentle humor that he uses to delight audiences and readers around the world.

A recovering restaurateur, a devoted husband and a pretty good Dad, Scott is happiest driving his pickup truck around beautiful downtown Center Point, Texas. It's not much but it is home! Scott likes planes, trains, and magic, and he has enough frequent flyer miles to trade for his own 737!

Life and business took a dramatic, positive turn when Scott discovered that when you are doing it right, work is fun. And that's his message for you: work hard, serve hard, have fun...and don't forget to love one another!

To enjoy Scott in person, call Tony Colao, Director, MasterMedia Speakers' Bureau at (800) 453-2887.

LEADING YOUR POSITIVELY OUTRAGEOUS SERVICE TEAM

T. SCOTT GROSS

MASTERMEDIA LIMITED
NEW YORK

Library of Congress Cataloging-in-Publication Date
Gross, T. Scott.
        Leading Your POSitively Outrageous
Service Team / T. Scott Gross.
        p. cm.
        ISBN
        #######
#######
########

Production services by Martin Cook Associates, Ltd.
Designed by Michael Woyton
Manufactured in the United States of America
10 9 8 7

CONTENTS

FOREWARD

The excitement of the next ten to twenty years will be centered around the tremendous opportunities that change brings. The growth of the services industry, the expansion of communications and information technology, globalized economies, corporate re-engineering, medical research break-throughs, demographic changes, transportation enhancements, and more will create whole new windows of opportunities for all of us.

T. Scott Gross presents the future to us in a way that takes away the blinders, the fear and expands our horizons and enthusiasm for meeting the challenges of change, with an optimistic confidence that can help us all position ourselves to maximize the opportunities.

Back in 1843, a manager with the U.S. Patent Office in Washington, D.C., decided to quite his position. In his letter of resignation, he stated that anything worth inventing had already been invented and patented. That was before the automobile, radio, television, computers, airplanes, cameras, plastic, microchips, fax machines, electric lights, motion pictures, videos, typewriters, word processors, X-rays, MRIs, submarines and satellites!

All this, and the best is yet to come! With Scott's vision, we all can enjoy the ride and the opportunities even more.

Mike McClelland
President/CEO
Hardware Wholesalers, Inc.

Introduction

There was only one reason for writing this book. It needed to be written.

We've spent the past few years telling the world about a marvelous brand of customer service that we named Positively Outrageous Service (POS). Audiences across the continent have laughed their way through our seminars and in many cases called for return engagements.

We've had cards and letters, photographs and video tapes from happy people who have either just discovered the joy of giving POS or who were simply grateful that someone would write a book that in some small way gave them both permission and explanation for some of the mondo-bizzarro things that they have done to surprise and delight their customers.

But, and this "but" is a big one, if there has been one question asked over and over, it has been this..."How do I get other people to follow me?"

This book is for all the folks who love customers and who have led the charge toward better service only to turn around and discover that they were alone.

This book is for the frantic executive who read my first book, *Positively Outrageous Service*, and then called to ask why he seemed to be the only person in his international organization willing to actually give it a try.

It is for another executive-friend who took over a large corporation with every intention of changing it to be a customer-focused, service powerhouse only to discover that the inherited culture of politics and backbiting was working against his every move. Well, this book's just what the doctor ordered.

And if you are truly a believer that customer service is *the* competitive advantage of our time, this book is for you.

Bonus...since Leading a Positively Outrageous Service Team should be fun, you can count on this book to be fun. So, get reading so you can get started!

PART I

TRENDS, TEAMS AND TECHNOLOGY

1

CAUGHT BETWEEN A ROCK
AND A HARD DRIVE

There is no point in creating a Positively Outrageous Service culture if it will be obsolete in the morning. Today's managers cannot remain lost in the past days of the 1950s, 1960s, 1970s or even 1980s, and expect to captain vibrant, successful organizations.

No, these are times when change is breaking across the bow of the corporate ship like so many waves on a windy day. These are times when corporate captains spend most of their time watching from the bow, looking for change to bring either opportunity or disaster.

We all know someone who simply refuses to use an ATM. We all know someone willing to trace the decline of civility to the introduction of answering machines and their offspring from hell, voice-mail systems. Most of the folks in charge of corporate America remember when corporate America was white, Anglo-Saxon and very, very male. And for a trip down memory lane, step into the nearest school or county courthouse where typewriters may still rule the desktop.

But, nevertheless, the future is arriving with incredible speed today. "In fact, change is happening so rapidly," according to futurist Edie Weiner, "it's like being Captain Kirk on the Starship Enterprise. When he hits warp-speed six, it's a geometric increase in the speed of the vehicle. Change happens so quickly, that he's going into another warp-speed and he doesn't feel it. That's what's happening to us today."

In the old days, and you can decide when that was, we had something called the "generation gap." You don't hear the term all that often any more and there's a reason.

Today, if you have children in third grade and their teacher is well-informed, they are learning to think about generations in an entirely new way. Generations are no longer defined in terms of time.

We used to think that a new generation was born each time the children of the present generation reached maturity and began to have children of their own. And that gentle rhythm of change coincided just nicely with the rate of other changes in technology and society. But today things are definitely different.

Today there are two ways to define a generation. First, the traditional definition linked to cycles of birth and death. The second way of defining a generation is to look at value systems. The reason you don't hear that term "generation gap" often is that with the startling increase in the rate of change, both technological and sociological, sociologists are now able to declare a new generation every four years. This means that it is likely that even most siblings are not of the same generation! That is because, thanks to television and other forms of mass communication, fads, trends, and other forces that shape our thoughts and values are now transmitted and assimilated at the speed of light.

For example, Weiner notes that the incredible advances in genetic engineering with the mapping of the human genetic code were startling, major front-page news just 20 years ago. "Now, new advances of this nature are often on page 17."

As just one sign of the rapidly diminishing length of a generation, country radio stations that identify themselves as playing "contemporary music" cut from their playlists anything that was recorded prior to 1987. (This is written in mid-1994 and already that cutoff date is moving closer to 1988.) Get it? Seven years after publication and music is fit only for stations playing "oldies?" The point is simply this: the waves of change are coming harder and faster and threaten to roll right over the executive who thinks an organization can exist in a technological and sociological vacuum.

When Alexander created his great library, there were less than a thousand written manuscripts to collect. Not to minimize what will always be a great feat, but imagine the impossibility of such a task today when, by some estimates, there are nearly one thousand books published every week. No comment about quality but, good Lord, look at the quantity! And that doesn't include the untold numbers of works created in other media such as tape, CD and software.

A NEW AGE SIX-PAK

Why don't people embrace change? Why don't they look at the new technology, listen to new ideas and simply burst with excitement? Why do people carry the music of their formative years throughout their lives? Simple. People like things that are familiar. The familiar makes them feel comfortable. And change is anything but comforting to most folks.

But to those who can embrace change and ride it like an industrial surfer, change will be the key to prosperity.

Weiner notes that,"the cycle of change is heating up for corporations and individuals." Her advice: "Never stop your education. Enterprising individuals have to rewire themselves to constantly sell and market to their corporation or others."

The other day, a visitor asked about our business. Melanie started into her answer by saying, "We're in transition...." Well, I can't remember when we haven't been "in transition!" Would you want to do serious business with an organization that wasn't?

In most any industry, there are those who look at change and say, "Don't tell me. I've been in this business for thirty years...."

Okay, big fella. Have you really been in the business thirty years or have you been in the business for one year thirty times?

Whatever the case, people don't change because they do what brought them to the party in the first place, afraid to change the magic formula that meant success in early days even if it's holding failure in place today.

We think about change. We talk about change. In the end, most of us, except for the winners who are ready to take intelligent risk, hold on to our old ideas and habits.

Weiner added, "Change imposes change. Our corporations are changing. The body of knowledge learned in college will not hold anyone in any profession, occupation, job or career today."

A FEW GOOD HINTS ABOUT TOMORROW

In no particular order, here is our forecast for the future of business in the U.S. and Canada.

In looking at the trends, we had difficulty separating one from the other. Indeed, they are all so interrelated that they could easily be discussed at once. In the interest of clarity, we present the following trend-composites, six sets of comments that look at today's hottest, most-likely-to-have-major-impact trends. Remember, please, that these are not predictions. They are a scouting report of what you, too, can see if you are willing to peek just this side of the horizon.

Techno-sizing	**Info-rush**
New Society	**The Tactical Prosumer**
Millenium Leader	**Solo Team**

2 ───────────────────────────────

THE MASTER TREND...
TECHNO-SIZING

*Synopsis: The way that work is being organized is changing
dramatically...and so are we!*

Techno-sizing is a local response to a global trend, the trend of technology making it ever easier to communicate and create products and services.

When Tom Curley, CEO and publisher of *USA Today*, is looking into the future, smart folks edge a little closer for a better view of the crystal ball. You know *USA Today*. It's that multi-zillion dollar Gannett gamble that finally proved that business travel and corporate communications would bring a sense of community to the entire country. You read it when Marriott or Holiday Inn slips it under your door. You make fun of it, but feel left out if you don't get your daily news fix while traveling.

The folks who created *USA Today* looked into the future and saw it clearly while the rest of the newspaper world was laughing. Of course, the rest of the newspaper business practically isn't, so what did they know? Certainly not what the future and technology could or would bring to their industry.

Curley and I shared a platform at the Mississippi Economic Development Symposium in beautiful Hattiesburg one warm spring day. It was too warm to listen but everyone did. Curley didn't make it two breaths into his speech before saying, "There is one economic imperative...

productivity." The audience had been hoping for something more high–tech, something more surprising. At first they probably decided that Curley wasn't much of a speaker. Then he repeated himself and either confirmed their suspicions or earned their attention.

It is "productivity that leads to growth...more output from less input."

In a few words, Curley had given body to one of the biggest trends anywhere, certainly one of the hottest buzzwords..."down-sizing." Aka, "right-sizing."

But we're going to call it "techno-sizing" because it is not one trend but many. It is not a fad although it is often treated as one. Techno-sizing is the automating of business made possible by the magic of silicon technology. Techno-sizing is right-sizing with a twist. It's more than getting small. It's getting small through innovative use of technology and management without cutting into sales or production. In fact, techno-sizing usually is accomplished by companies that are increasing market share and profitability.

Techno-sizing has nothing to do with cost-cutting although that is one inevitable result. No, techno-sizing is the combined trends of right-sizing, that is engineering the job to be more productive, often eliminating unnecessary steps while moving simultaneously to an increasing dependence on electronic technology to improve the efficiency of the portions of the process that remain. Whew! 'Lotta words and we need more.

Techno-sizing is one trend made possible by another.

Had there been no electronic revolution, there would be no re-engineering of the scale that we are seeing today.

All sorts of formerly critical steps in the production of products and services are being eliminated. Not because they were never necessary but because new technology has provided shortcuts that, to the customer, don't seem like shortcuts at all.

For example, one company that went to the post office in the 1970s to pick up orders was by the 1980s receiving them by an 800-number. Within a matter of a few short years, the 800-number had been supplemented by a fax machine. By the early 1990s, key customers were entering their own orders via electronic data exchange.

By reordering the way basic information is handled, businesses can hardly avoid reorganizing...work gets done. I don't know who first noticed, but one huge trend of the moment is the trend toward flattened organizational structures. Middle management has become increasingly irrelevant. The job of most middle managers has traditionally been to serve as a communications conduit or filter between the honchos at the top and the workers in the trenches. The analogy to the military is more than obvious, it is perfect.

Recently the Pentagon announced that it would be spending *five-hundred million dollars* for the development of flat- screen video technology. At first it seems odd that the military would be so interested in developing a technology that would put large, flat video screens on the wall of every home, office and public space. But while flat-screen technology may seem ideally suited to entertainment and newscasting, it has even more uses on the battlefield.

The Pentagon is looking for technology that will allow it to build video screens into the helmets of soldiers, aviators and weapons teams.

Think about it. Instant, graphic, visual communication. So who needs middle management?

Firefighters, SWAT teams, even medical personnel operating in remote areas of the country will be able to take advantage of database information and expert advice located many thousands of miles distant.

If all this is too much like Star Wars or Star Trek, just look around you right now. Unless you are reading from a mountaintop or remote, deserted island, chances are good that you have one or more microprocessor-controlled devices within reach. Isn't that amazing? A little piece of technology that didn't exist more than a few decades ago has finally found its place into nearly every human activity.

What is important for this discussion is not the spread of technology nor even that technology has and will continue to make humans even more efficient killers. What is important is that technology is having a profound impact on the organization of the workforce. As the ability of top management to communicate directly with those who actually perform the service or produce the product increases, there will be less and less need for middle managers.

Why do you suppose that the economy of the early nineties failed to bounce back as it had after every other economic downturn? Why did we see sales improve but not overall employment, especially among white-collar workers? Because we are in the middle of a new industrial revolution where not only is the worker more efficient, he or she is also less likely to be directly supervised. (Thank or curse technology for this.)

We recently made a presentation to a major insurance company and were not surprised to learn that over the past few years, they had added considerably to their claims processing staff. Over the same period, the ranks of supervisory staff had actually declined. In fact, the ratio of supervisors to clerks had declined from 1:7 to better than 1:22. This is not what you would call an exceptional case. Technology has dramatically increased what the military first called a supervisor's "span of control."

Middle managers are now an endangered species.

Techno-sizing has been more about figuring how to get rid of expensive layers of middle managers than about anything else. If you accept the idea that the primary purpose of middle managers is to control, process and filter communication between the top and the bottom of an organization, it should be no surprise that once the top and bottom can communicate freely and instantly, there is little need for a middle manager.

Once the big guys started to cut, they made another surprising discovery. Much of the layering that they were trying to eliminate had absolutely nothing to do with core processes.

Once business leaders began to look for excess fat, they saw it everywhere they looked. They began to realize that many in-house service providers had been hired more out of convenience and empire building than out of real business necessity. Departments, such as graphic design, marketing, legal and even product development and training, could, in many cases, be eliminated. Their services, like the small parts and assemblies already targeted by manufacturing groups could also be out-sourced.

Upon closer inspection, it seemed likely that a company could save considerably by paying outside vendors to provide non-core-related products and services as needed. This was true even in cases where outside vendors charged a higher rate since they would only be paid for the duration of the project instead of being a constant drain on the payroll.

A side benefit was this: outside vendors of non-core-related products and services would bring with them the expertise gained from working on projects in other industries. When businesses intentionally look outside their home industry for solutions, the process is called parallel analysis. By out-sourcing services in addition to products, companies also, although usually unknowingly, begin to benefit from new ideas that crawl in over the transom.

If techno-sizing is the master trend, then what are its offspring?

LET'S GET REEEALLY SMALL

Now, thanks to technology, the big boys are losing the advantage of size. Size in many instances has become a near liability. When the product is a knowledge-based product, there isn't much value in the reduced costs of coordinating materials and assets that yesterday's behemoth used to consider its competitive advantage. Many of today's most profitable and sought-after products have very little mass indeed. Isn't that true for software, networking and tele–communications industries, the fastest growing industries around?

You might think that corporate information workers would be the least likely to be cut in an information age. Wrongo! Secretaries, the number one corporate information workers, have seen their job ranks hacked away like so much kudzu under a highway mower. As recently as 1987, there were 4.1 million secretaries looking for respect and parity and getting little of either.

Today there are fewer than 3.5 million, and I guarantee you that, for the most part, they have been accepted as the professionals they are.

If techno-sizing is about anything, it is the way that we handle communication. Look at today's top executives and you'll look over the top of their CRT or notebook computer. Today's busy exec inputs communication directly, no fussing over dictation or handwritten notes.

The big news is not that executives are lousy keyboardists, they are. The big news is that it is this direct involvement with manipulating data that has resulted in the demise of middle management. The very function of middle management was to handle or interpret communication between the ivory tower and the troops on the line. Not necessary any longer.

Several years ago we made a presentation to the executives at AAFES (Army/Air Force Exchange Service), one of the largest retailers in the world. They sell everything from soup to nuts, tires to ties at military installations world–wide. And when the head honcho wants to know about yesterday's sales of Whoppers at the franchised unit on the island of Guam, he doesn't have to scout out a mid–level manager to call for the numbers.

A few clicks on his desktop keyboard and the numbers are there. It's the mid-level manager who is gone.

If you are in mid-level management, this is not a happy chapter for you. If you haven't seen the writing on the wall and your boss isn't showing signs of retiring...get the picture? On the other hand, it is this kind of effective use of technology that keeps costs down. Today's corporation is focusing resources on the customer like a laser. No unnecessary energy or resource is wasted on tending bureaucracy or feeding extravagant perks. (Perks, these days, are being lavished on the true organization heroes, the folks with the most customer contact.)

In all the frenzy to right-size, large corporations are discovering that size is often a disadvantage. They are breaking large organizations into small units run with an entrepreneurial spirit and freedom. For once, the big guys are looking enviously at the little guys who are eating their lunch!

The middle managers are doing what they've always done. They are doing the hard work of supporting the core competencies, only now they do the job while working as independent contractors, often for the large companies that forced them into early retirement. We have a relative who worked for twenty-plus years for AT&T. He spent the last ten of those years asking for lateral promotions every two years. This was his strategy for avoiding becoming too conspicuous and having to face the axe before he was emotionally and financially ready.

When the axe did fall, he accepted early retirement and immediately took a job as a consultant for, you guessed it, AT&T. Higher pay, lower benefits. But essentially the same job.

AT&T had the concept of right-sizing even though they didn't execute all that admirably.

Futurist Marvin Cetron, in his landmark work *American Renaissance*, said that as the revolution unfolds "mid-size institutions will vanish...thousands of tiny companies will flourish." This will occur as companies right-size, sending their most competent but unneeded mid-level managers into consultancies and the least competent or daring into unemployment, early retirement or into jobs for which they are overqualified.

The rapid advancement of high–tech has created an imperative for business and a disaster for workers.

As competition has reduced costs by reducing labor and cutting out unneccessary procedures, technology has become a do–or–die proposition. Usually it's only a matter of acquiring off–the–shelf technology and putting it to work. Suddenly we are faced with an army of displaced workers.

Unlike the transition to other technologies where displaced workers could be retrained and charged with the operation and maintenance of the new hardware, this time, workers are being permanently displaced. Because this time around, technology does more than streamline operations...it eliminates them. No need to retrain.

Technology is allowing business to shed workers, lower costs and increase output. And technology can be acquired faster than the economy can grow. The worry is that we could easily find ourselves with a super-efficient economy and no customers. Sort of all dressed up and no place to go.

AT&T, for example, used new switching technology to drop from forty-four thousand long distance operators to fifteen thousand almost overnight. Imagine the surprise of those displaced operators. Who could have dreamed that that they could be replaced so quickly, if at all?

PacBell began an experiment in an attempt to get a handle on the rapidy rising cost of repair service. When the cost of dispatching a truck to a residence rose to $140 a shot, someone thought that there has to be a better way.

And there was. A computer diagnostic routine was developed that allowed the company to reduce the number of truck dispatches by 30 percent, no mean savings unless you are one of the repair operatives displaced by a box of chips and solder. And who would have thought that an on–the–site repair person could ever be replaced? Made more efficient, perhaps. But replaced? Never!

Wrong.

"High–tech makes it possible for business to shed workers faster than they must be rehired to manage the technology or support expanding sales." So says the *Wall Street Journal* in what must be the understatement of the decade.

TECHNO-SIZING

What is the real secret behind the new technology? What does it do that makes this evolution more revolution?

First, with the new technology, we are learning to reach not across geographic boundaries but corporate boundaries. When computers began to creep their way into organizations, they were initially used for the same functions as the older technology whose desk space they had captured. Typewriters went the way of word processors. Copy machines were replaced by laser printers. And productivity gained was productivity lost to reading the impossible manuals that came with the software!

But finally it happened. We discovered that computers could be used to communicate. Information that once took an Act of Congress to pry out of the MIS department could now be made available at the touch of a key, or two. In spite of the fact that business is using more paper than ever, the tide has begun to turn.

In our own small office, telephone messages are no longer passed around on small scraps of paper. There are few handwritten notes or memos. Team members work from their homes, some at great distance but all can easily communicate via modem and e-mail. Schedules that once took forever to coordinate can now be done in a matter of minutes.

Most important is the leveling effect that e-mail has on office relationships. On the e-mail screen, the chairperson looks identical to the stockroom supervisor. There is something magic about the ability to communicate in the relative anonymity of electronic cyberspace. There are no fancy offices to intimidate, no dress-code barriers, or language which can be difficult to handle when you are sweating over an audience with the big boss. It takes on a relaxed flavor of its own when allowed to percolate through a revision or two.

And, with few restrictions, every employee can have available the same operating information as the boss. That's democracy!

How big is the electronic revolution? For the first time in history, in 1991, business spent more on information technology than on "old economy" equipment. There is the signal you've been waiting for; the information age has arrived. It is the biggest trend since electricity. And as the technology grows, you can count on business to be ever more creative at using it to replace more expensive tools and talent.

Already we have seen technology impact the economy in massive ways. The recession of the early 1990s seemed to linger long past its expected departure. It did. Only because there were more than the usual forces at work correcting for inflation and high interest rates. This time the economy was also in the midst of a technology revolution that contributed to the demise not of the usual bottom of the barrel layoffs but to the massive dislocation of mid-level white-collar management.

Technology had finally arrived in force to change the way work gets done. This time though, technology was impacting not just the efficiency of individual work processes but the way work processes are organized. Now comes the bittersweet fruit of all this investment in electronic technology. Over the past ten years while Fortune 500 companies have reduced employment by 20 percent, investment technology has tripled! This means that productivity has never been higher.

HORIZONTALLY, YOURS

It is technology that allows business to reorganize production around markets rather than products or functions. In the early days, there was mass production. A product was created and the sales force sent out to find a buyer. Costs went down when production runs grew longer. The biggest avoidable expense was retooling, which meant that production had to stop, and labor dollars were spent to reconfigure the line for a different product.

Today, the idea of mass production has given way to the idea of mass customization. Thanks to computerized controls, we can have the benefit of long production runs while at the same time customizing every unit produced.

This capability brings with it a new form of stress. The customer begins to expect customization. The customer no longer is willing to settle for limited selection. They want it their way...and they don't expect to wait!

To answer the call of and for mass customization, organizations are reorganizing more horizontally, putting to work cross-functional teams that represent many departments. The idea is to define the market, then define the product. Departments work in parallel to create prototype products ready for manufacture without costly, time-consuming re-engineering required to make it cost-effective to produce. The prototype is often the final product.

The horizontal organization often invites customers to be directly involved in the creation of the product. These organizations look to the customer instead of looking to the boss as they eliminate department and functional boundaries.

SELF-DIRECTED TEAMS

Horizontal organizations can't be run like traditional vertical organizations. What makes them special, the reason they work is that traditional political I'm-the-boss-wait-for-me decision-making has been eliminated or at least minimized. The work of tomorrow will be done by teams, teams that consist of professionals who are treated like professionals. These teams will be largely self-directed, every manager's dream until it happens.

We're talking empowerment here and this is, to many managers, definitely risky territory. Few organizations will be true horizontal organizations. Most will be a hybrid to one degree or another.

Not every worker is suited for the empowering environment of self-directed work teams. The players will be different. Those who have never learned or been allowed to use their brains simply will not fit this new environment without some serious adaptation. That's okay. There will continue to be many organizations that will run on the old model. Employees who need to be bossed rather than led can still find a home.

Self-directed teams require self-directed players.

These players actually want freedom, (not always the same as authority.) Most important, they want ownership. Of the process. Of their time. Of the company! Smart managers will find ways to grant ownership without losing control.

If you are not already feeling threatened, try this. In truly empowered organizations, the customer is also empowered to shape the process. As the trend to get horizontal continues to develop, companies are discovering that the customer must be included early and throughout the process.

At the end of the process, customers are left to rummage, usually electronically, through companies' stockrooms as they place orders, check inventory levels and shipping status.

DYNAMIC TEAMS

Teams will be dynamic in nature, usually assembled for targeted projects. Once the project has been completed, the team will disband. Players will be reassigned to new teams or devote more time to other teams of which they are members. Although players may have multiple team assignments, each team is likely to be working on only one tightly focused project at a time.

Managers of self-directed teams will play a vastly different role from the traditional. They will, as does a traditional manager, assemble the team, looking for the right combination of talent and personality. Once the team is formed, the role changes dramatically.

Team managers will also be team players. Perhaps they will have been selected for their ability to contribute a key, call it "vocational", skill to the team mix. It is also likely that team managers will command no greater pay or status than other members of the team.

Team managers will serve in one of two newly titled functions: team owner and the rather revolutionary idea of team champion. Team owners will be responsible for the day-to-day functioning of the team. Team owners may or may not participate on a regular basis but they will be expected to be closely connected to the work and goals of the team, for it is the duty of the team champion to keep the team linked to the strategy and goals of the entire organization.

Team champions have the job of making certain that the team has the physical, financial and political resources necessary to succeed.

The idea of "boss" has pretty much gone out the window...in the case of self-managed teams.

Self-directed teams have a number of advantages. First and foremost is that players have a sense of control and ownership that almost guarantees improved results. Because team players are so personally linked to the outcome, there is a strong pride of craft not usually seen where employees are asked to tighten a bolt or install a widget to something that simply gets passed along the line.

Teams present a strong, positive peer pressure, creating buy-in often more out of concern about letting the team down than over the product itself.

Of course, there is nothing that replaces the satisfaction of seeing a project through from conception to delivery. And there is the joy of synergy that inevitably results when folks are encouraged to collaborate. The result is what Stewart Brand, creator of the Whole Earth Catalogue, calls "scenius", the genius of collective creativity.

Sunbeam-Oster carries the idea of self-directed work teams right to the production floor where teams of operatives work in "clusters" to build small appliances. These workers are not drawn from the ranks of the well-educated or specially trained. They are ordinary Americans who live and work in Hattiesburg, Miss., and prove everyday that genius can be found anywhere management will take the time to look.

OUT-SOURCING

As companies focus more tightly on the customer, they will inevitably discover that they have, over the years, taken on support departments that no longer make sense to keep in an organization that is streamlining in areas representing core competencies.

As sales, production and shipping departments come under review for cost-effectiveness, departments such as training, marketing, accounting and others will eventually fall under the harsh glare of the auditor's spotlight.

Organizations will continue the trend of focusing on core competencies and out-source everything else. The result will be that as companies right-size and work in core competency areas with fluid or dynamic teams, they will begin to form similar relationships with a cadre of regular suppliers. There will be more supplier loyalty at least in non-core competency areas as small suppliers become, in a sense, the training, marketing or accounting departments of their client companies. Some will even establish offices at or very near client locations.

So what is the difference in bringing the function in-house? You only pay for the service when you need it. The vendor has the responsibility to keep up with the latest in their field of expertise. And whatever you out-source is not your field of expertise. The organization is left to focus on those ever-important core competencies. Oil companies are not trying to manage exploration and refining while at the same time are building in-house printing plants, video production facilities and other non-core distractions. Instead they are tightly focused on finding, recovering and refining crude. That's what they do best.

In fact, three of ten companies out-source more than half of their manufacturing. Get it? There are even core competencies of core competencies! Where a company may have a strong ability to design, it may have a weakness in the manufacture of certain portions of their own product. This is natural especially if new technology that is outside the original set of competencies is incorporated into new designs.

Companies that apply their core competencies to new products usually command higher markups and gain market share. So it is logical to focus on design and production in core areas and out-source that which is not a strong suit. Thanks to technology it is now easier than ever to coordinate with outside vendors to create a seamless interface with in-house needs.

DISINTERMEDIATION!

Disintermediation. It's the biggest word I know but also one of the most critical for business to understand. It is the process of removing the middle man.

Disintermediation, a concept first named formally by Stanley Davis in his book, *Future Perfect*, is made possible by technology.

We've been talking around the concept of disintermediation, now let's look at it squarely. When technology allows us to communicate more effectively across organizational boundaries, we are disintermediating. Sounds sexy and it is, so long as you are not the mid-level manager who is displaced. And sexy, so long as your entire organization is not displaced as happens when giant retailers purchase directly from the manufacturer, cutting out the wholesaler and jobber/distributor.

The more intermediary the job or organization, the more vulnerable it will be to being shortcut.

When disintermediation occurs, space is created for other activities such as focusing on those all-important core competencies. Small businesses are already, by nature, disintermediated. The boss is doing things that in large business would be done by a support department. Of course, that takes her away from focus on core competencies, too, so there is a push-pull between seeking to down-size and searching for economies of scale.

What techno-sizing has done is to bring economy to much smaller scale.

3

INFO-RUSH

*Synopsis: The information age is more than upon us. It is us.
Products without mass are the new stars of commerce.*

Tom Curley observes that the top growth industries are software, networking and tele–communications. Sure they are. What else brings so much added productivity per dollar invested? And look at the thousands of innovative uses of technology that are popping up everywhere.

Remember when the Wizard of Avis was an electronic miracle? Avis could rent a car in a matter of minutes with its marvelous automated terminal. Today such technology is no longer a marvel; it is mandatory! In the car rental business, you have to have great technology just to get into the game. Now Alamo, Dollar and most of the other players are using portable computer equipment to provide instant check in when you return the vehicle. They print your receipt from a unit worn on the waist. Now that's technology!

Three of ten American homes have a computer. Do you remember when a visit would sometimes result in an invitation to "see our new computer?" You would be stuck for hours in front of a monochrome screen watching DOS prompts and praying for relief of any kind, even vacation slides! Today, almost everyone who reads this book has a computer.

Forty percent of all computers are networked. That means that the computer is no longer a piece of equipment. It is a social instrument that connects people to data and people to people.

Data traffic carried by telephone lines is growing at a rate of 30 percent per year. Americans may account for only 23 percent of the world's GDP but we are at the other end of 68.1 percent of the world's electronic mailboxes!

The average home has about one hundred embedded controller chips in its appliances, automobiles, communications and entertainment devices up from six in 1980, a big fat zero in 1970...and we're on our way to an incredible three hundred by the turn of the century!

Employees who use a computer on the job have increased from 24.6 percent in Orwell's famous year, 1984, to more than 40 percent today.

VCRs have multiplied like electronic rabbits growing from eight million in 1983 to an astonishing seventy million a mere decade later! Microwaves have become common. They are in 70 percent of American homes. CDs have found their way into our homes by the millions. Four hundred million are produced every year. That's quite a jump from the one million that were pressed in 1983.

And cellular phones? Take a guess. Would you believe eleven million, not much more than a decade after their introduction?

Today we are scrambling to find our financial, industrial, social and emotional footholds in a world that has undergone unexpected revolution. We didn't think that the wave of technology would so quickly and thoroughly encompass us. Each change seemed ubiquitous by itself. But together they have left us living in a drastically changed environment.

If we imagine that no more change is on the way, we will surely drown in our own invention.

What's coming?

Object-oriented programming (OOP), that promises to dramatically decrease the time and effort required to create new programs. OOP consists of high-powered reuseable program modules. By using these prefabricated blocks of program power, programmers should see an incredible increase in productivity and users will see the price of programs fall dramatically.

Pen-based programs will allow users to communicate directly with their computers in writing. I believe that this new technology will be bypassed in favor of the even easier to use-voice recognition. Already we are seeing Murphy Brown touting the voice recognition features offered by Sprint. Can voice recognition for the home and office be far away?

One hot dream bound to change the world will be realized when the VCR and the home computer become one and the same animal. The key to this lies in the simplicity of the interface. Make it easy for anyone to use a computer and watch the barriers fall. Along with this development must come the one button remote control/mouse. It will come and when it does the information highway will run through every living room in the civilized world.

As technology becomes more portable entire neighborhoods will change. The days when someone was home for the kids will return—not because more women will stay at home to watch the children but because more people, men and women, will stay at home to work.

Bill Gates of Microsoft dreams of taking the computer off the desk and putting it into the pocket, onto the wrist or even into the wallet. As computing power becomes more mobile and allows us in turn to be more mobile, the power of the info-rush will be ours.

4

SOLO TEAM

Synopsis: *Tomorrow's most successful corporations will be sole proprietors that look and behave like a typical employee but will be neither typical nor an employee.*

The Rise of the Professional Contingent Worker.

We've heard about it but without hearing it. We've known it was happening without realizing that it was at last upon us.

The trend? The rise of the professional contingent worker. As big as the trend of hiring, even leasing workers may be, the trend of hiring temporary professional employees is even greater.

Attorneys, paramedicals, designers, programmers and highly-skilled maintenance technicians are among the professional workers that are being placed along with the secretaries and stock clerks that we traditionally think of as being the mainstay of the temporary workforce.

A client of ours, Imprimis of Dallas, Texas, has responded to the demand for professionals capable of handling temporary graphic arts assignments. Imprimis has created a whole new division called "The Art Squad."

Think about it. Here we have a temporary workforce for an industry that only a decade ago did not even exist in its present form.

Another client, Pro Staff, is working to create a similar niche product that promises to be so successful that we can't discuss it here. But the point should be unmistakable...professional contingent workers are a wave of the future.

Already nearly 65 percent of the American workforce is involved in service, technical or knowledge industries, a number that is bound to grow as the high-tech future unfolds.

Thanks to the fact that computers are absolutely everywhere, agencies that provide contingent workers are now offering employees designated by their proficiency with specific software programs. The contingent worker of today no longer is looked to as a strong back and weak mind hired to hold down a telephone or unload a truck. Today the contingent worker may come from an agency or be a one woman, home-based company. Whatever the case, while the demand for employees capable of manual labor has not dried up completely, the demand for contingent knowledge workers has soared.

And the smart money says the trend will continue.

In many cases, companies that have "right-sized" often end up hiring as contingent workers the very persons who they had laid off in the first place. And why not? These folks are already trained and ready to work, often being fired one day and rehired on a contract basis the very next.

For the company the arrangement works just fine. They get a well-seasoned employee without the obligation to contribute further to retirement and other expenses. The employee wins, too. The comfort of an assured retirement and the freedom to leave should job conditions become unsatisfactory are side benefits that although difficult to measure, are big draws to participants.

One key word, in case you missed it, is the word "professional." As companies take the idea of techno-sizing to its logical extreme, there will be more and more pressure for contingent workers to be even better than regular team players.

Increasingly, we may become a nation of small businesses that could accurately be named, You, Inc., as corporations techno-size and displaced workers hang out their own shingles. For those who remain, a variation on the theme may well arise for intrapreneurs, team players who have been given both stake and go-ahead to create organizations within larger parent companies.

The parent companies will be those which have realized that, in many cases, small really is beautiful. They will become incubators for those with entrepreneurial spirit, encouraging them to grow profits for the company rather than take their ideas and become competitors.

Even employees who are more comfortable in the role of follower may have to adjust to new ways of work. For many, the idea of a regular job with nine-to-five hours and predictable duties will become a thing of the past. This will happen as organizations attempt to respond to the needs of the customer for service outside the bounds of "normal" work hours and place.

The hospitality industry has understood the idea of playing to the customer since the beginning of time. We would never say to a customer, "Could you come back sometime Monday through Friday between nine and five? Our employees would prefer to have their weekends to themselves."

Imagine a restaurant trying to pull that!

One inescapable though disappointing trend is the trend toward eliminating full-time jobs in favor of part-time workers. Part-timers get few if any benefits and in return owe precious little loyalty. This is a trend that is not good for America. It creates a vast pool of contingent though hardly professional workers.

As more and more businesses begin to put the service desires of their customers first, we'll see the idea of nine-to-five go straight out the window. We'll all be contingent workers of a sort.

As techno-sizing gains momentum, it promises to be a way of life for a very long time. Organizations themselves may appear, grow, prosper and then give way to new technology or reinvent themselves as technology and the market changes. Some of our oldest institutions have done just that over a matter of decades. In the future, such rapid evolution may need to be a key part of any organization's strategic plan.

Paul Meunier, of Signature Flight Support, based in Orlando, Fla., once told me that his team could run almost any business successfully; it just happened that they were in air transport. It could just as easily have been any other endeavor requiring teamwork and creativity. Maybe that's the next idea on the horizon, the contingent team!

THE RISE OF THE PLAID-COLLAR WORKER

As long as we're hiring contingent, professional workers, why not look at what this means to how and where people will work and live?

We believe that technology will do more than allow people to work at home. It will change where they choose to live. With a fax and a modem, perhaps throw in a toll-free number, a business could conceivably locate anywhere.

Land's End is probably the premier example of a business that packed up and headed for the heartland. It's slick catalogue and quality merchandise make Land's End a winner of a business. And being located in the boonies doesn't hurt; it actually helps.

With the U.S. Postal Service, UPS and Federal Express reaching nearly every inch of the country, as long a there is a quality telephone line in the area, there is little or no limit on where a business can locate. For experts connected to the information superhighway, the world is their market, not just the friendly folks who live within a 2.5 mile radius. And the start-up cost for a technology-supported information business is nominal.

Within five miles of this word processor, there is a manufacturer of high-tech aerospace products, a computer programmer, a big-city homicide detective, several oil field consultants and who knows what kind of talent. Within three feet of this word processor lies an all-white German Shepherd wearing a snazzy teddy bear scarf! Connected to this word processor (a Dell 486 color jobbie) is a rather sophisticated computer network supported by a former college professor who, like the rest of us, has decided that when it comes to the big city, it just isn't worth the hassle.

This February, the big deal in town was the annual Lion's Club Pancake Supper. Rubbing shoulders in the crowded kitchen at the junior high school was a rather eclectic mix of farmers, ranchers, and a host of work-at-home professionals. The point? If you want to enjoy life in the country, come on down! We've got great schools with few of the problems experienced by big cities. We get our news via satellite, our croissants from the nearest superstore, our clothes are delivered to our unlocked door and we are home to receive them.

And you want to make fun of country folks? Think again.

The prediction is simple. As Americans discover the joy of working as contingent, electronic workers working from their homes, where those homes are located will increasingly be in rural areas. These new workers we call "Plaid-Collar Workers", folks who have turned in their suits and ties in favor of jeans and plaid shirts. Wingtips rarely hold out in the face of boots. Pickups are now as comfortable as the family sedan (and they hold a lot more!)

Small towns that had been suffering from a dramatic population loss are about to see an equally dramatic reversal. In *Megatrends 2000*, John Naisbett said that if cities didn't already exist, there would be no need to invent them. Amen.

As the new Plaid-Collar Worker heads to the hills, there will be an inevitable backlash from those who never left. Small town stores will find themselves needing to stock things that the locals consider so much froufrou. And those plaid-collar folks will just as inevitably bring with them the problems that they sought to escape. Their kids will bring with them the big-city styles and social habits that the locals have seen on TV, but managed to avoid mostly through the advantage of distance. Distance keeps the fads at bay, keeping them too far away to make that huge cultural leap.

But, the big city will eventually come to town.

And the country will have its share of influence on those left to gut it out in the smog and traffic, the coffee bars and malls.

As the Plaid-Collar Worker becomes less and less of an exception, we'll see a change to a more rural, friendlier way of doing business. This will also begin to influence our big-city peers who at least dream of escaping crime and traffic. We are already seeing signs of this. Look at the popularity of safari clothes and hiking boots. And what about Ford Explorers and William Sonoma cookware? These may be a material representation of the desire to leave the city.

The Plaid-Collar Worker and the rise of the contingent, professional worker are major trends impacting more than from where we do business. These trends will change the way business gets done.

By the year 2000, it is estimated that 20 percent of the workforce will work at home. If that idea suits you, why aren't you working toward being in that 20 percent?

The new worker will bring with him or her a host of new problems. Not necessarily horrible social problems, but problems just the same. How will these new workers need to be managed? How will we keep track of them? Why will we want to?

We'll look for solutions in later chapters. For now, just remember, that as the world changes, the change will not always be a matter of a new box of technology.

New technology brings with it more than interesting gadgets. New technology changes more than the way work gets done; it changes the worker as well. It will be up to the new leader to show the world how to keep the peace between the technology we use and the people we want to become.

ONE FINAL LESSON

The future belongs to YOU. There will be no such thing as working for the same company for thirty years unless you own it and, guaranteed, even if you do own the company, what you end with will little resemble the one you started with. We will all be, in one way or another, contingent workers, loyal first to our own development.

To survive you must:

Think of yourself as a business.

Define your product.

Know who is your target market.

Discover your unique points of difference.

Be the best in your field.

Do your own product development...keep growing as a
  professional.

Be willing to change when the writing is on the wall.

Accept responsibility for your own career and retirement.

5

NEW SOCIETY

Synopsis: *If there is one thing that could stop our economy in its move to a new economic order, it will be our lack of social preparedness.*

There are two major trend areas that mark the new society and they are related. First, there are several disturbing trends in the family. Second, the new world, that techno-sized world that is coming soon, demands a new kind of learner. Lifelong learners will be required if we are to build a society that does not endure the ugly disparity between the haves and the have-nots that mark so many other parts of the world. So far, the news isn't good.

THE NEW LEARNER

The average high school student today knows little that will be valuable in the work world of tomorrow. Many have had little exposure to higher order thinking skills, principles of advanced mathematics or literature. Few who carry their degree from the podium are able to communicate well in English. As a nation, we are more than at risk; we are in deep kimchee.

At minimum, a graduating student should...

➤ Be able to communicate clearly both orally and in writing.
➤ Have a thorough background in history, geography and literature.

➤ Be able to apply basic math principles to everyday situations.

➤ Be a master of at least one foreign language.

➤ Have developed an appreciation for the fine arts.

➤ Have participated in at least one of the performing arts.

➤ Be computer literate.

➤ Understand how government works and his/her responsibility to participate.

➤ Be physically fit.

➤ Be capable of self-directed learning.

➤ Have experience working to solve problems as a team.

➤ Be experienced at using his/her imagination to solve problems.

Education should focus on those things done poorly by the computer. It should cease to focus on rote memorization and turn instead to the development of higher order thinking skills.

Students should be prepared to work as professional or technical workers since these are the fastest growing job types. They should also be well adept at working as a team—and we're not talking football! We're talking about the ability to contribute to a long-term problem solving exercise.

Unfortunately, not all that many students graduate. The drop-out rate in some communities exceeds 40 percent. What can business do with a high school drop out? Not much. But then, these citizens of the underclass rarely interface with business other than as customers anyway.

A postal carrier told me of delivering entitlement checks to a family where there are four sets of households receiving support of one kind or another. A 12-year-old girl took the mail one delivery day and turned to have her mother sign for delivery.

"You do it, honey," was the mother's reply. "You'll have to learn how to do that someday."

Sorry to lean again on Tom Curley but he said it so well. "Higher education, as we know it, will cease to exist. Large corporations will replace all but a few elite universities. The idea of a college campus is irrelevant to all but an 18-year-old and tenured professors."

Learning in the coming years will be a lifelong process. It will not take place with the exception on campus. We must be willing to seek out and embrace new ways of learning if we are to realize our full potential as an economy and as a people.

6

MILLENIUM LEADER

*Synopsis: The new leader will be like none that we've seen before.
Part cheerleader, part team player. And all visionary.*

INTELLIGENT RISK, FLEXIBLE, PASSION-CHARISMA, SERVANT-LEADER

Those are the four key traits that define the leader of the new millenium. In a new world, one that resembles but does not imitate that which has gone before, a new style of leadership must develop. The old ways of highly regimented, following of orders will disappear along with the autocratic leaders who insistently hang on until the entire organization gets eaten by the competition.

In their places will be another breed.

INTELLIGENT RISK

The late 1990s will be an entrepreneur's dream; plenty of opportunity to bid old ties *adieu* and strike out on one's own. Better yet, time to engineer that business unit that has been calling. Or if you are lucky enough to be the boss, time to take it to the highway and "see what this baby can do!"

Whatever the circumstance, it will require risk. Ask the folks who have gone before to tell you how it feels to work all hours of the day.

(This is being written at 7:22 on a beautiful summer's evening, that late time in the day when the deer begin to test the grass at the edge of the meadow; when wine tastes as if it were made from the sun. But here I sit, tip,tap,typing away. Resentful? Never! It's been years since I've kissed a corporate backside. I wouldn't trade freedom for all the fancy suits on Park Avenue!)

Ask them to tell you if, given a chance to change their mind, they would have chosen differently. "Sooner," is the only response you are likely to hear, even from the corporate types who traded the three-piece for a hat and apron to make sandwiches in their new franchise operation.

Great leaders are intelligent risk takers. They bet on themselves. They may bet on you. In the future, we'll need lots of folks who can spot an intelligent risk and move boldly, intuitively. The future will belong to those who make big, bold moves.

It takes guts to let team players make the big decisions. What if they screw up?

If they learn and it didn't cost the company, then chalk it up to training. If they didn't learn and it didn't cost much, it still cost too much.

FLEXIBILITY

The new leader must be flexible. Working with self-directed teams demands a recognition that there is more than one "right" answer. Leaders who give directions to the nth degree aren't leading at all, they are directing.

Self-directed teams will include players from several departments. Their leaders will have to be masters of handling interdepartmental sensitivities. If it sounds like corporate politics. It is. But flexible leaders with the organization's interests at heart will not make work issues into political contests.

Bill Oncken wrote about something called "Monkey Management." He said that when employees keep leaving monkeys (requests for decisions or other help) on your desk, it is a sign of poor management. In a well-led team, players solve problems on their own. They may ask for guidance or resources, but they don't leave the big stuff with the boss. Leaning on the boss is a sign of poor hiring, poor training or that the boss is a control freak.

All that is fine provided the boss is available every waking hour. Otherwise leaders need a technique to keep the monkeys off the desk. Oncken taught me this phrase, useful just about anytime you spot an employee about to deposit a big, fat, juicy monkey in your in-box.

Just say, "Hmmm, that's interesting. How are you going to handle that?"

Then you can enjoy the scene as your would-be day-killer walks from your office with a big one thoroughly screwed to his back!

Effective leaders of tomorrow will be flexible enough to let the teamwork...in their way.

PASSION-CHARISMA

The new leader must be a salesperson. A cheerleader of sorts. This is because self-directed teams of professionals don't want to be told, they want to be sold. The leader of the future may or may not have status or compensation that exceeds that of the other members of the team.

Think about that. The team leader or team owner may have been selected with the idea in mind that leader skills are just one more addition to the other skills the team will need to reach its goal.

Get it? We need someone who is good at marketing. A finance expert. Better include someone from MIS and, oh yes, don't forget to include someone to act as the leader. On self-directed teams and with contingent workers especially, everyone will be expected to exhibit leadership.

By the original definition, a leader is a horse harnessed first among others in the same hitch. Not out front. Not off to the side. Not sitting in a big, comfortable office. But first among others in the same hitch. The leader is a team player, a team member too.

SERVANT-LEADER

I love that term. It will be especially important as the decade continues to unfold. Customers are used to getting good service. Your team players are your customers. Good leaders are good servers. They put the team first.

Team players will treat their customers almost exactly like they are treated. Great service leaders are passing along great customer service through their treatment of the team.

7

THE TACTICAL PROSUMER

Synopsis: *There is an emerging new consumer. We met him first at a warehouse retailer. Now he is everywhere!*

Today's consumers are smarter than ever before. And why not? We've spent billions educating them! In fact, in the last ten years, ad spending per person has increased nearly 60 percent! Technology has brought an ever-increasing array of dazzling products that get cheaper by the moment.

Take the typical small hand tool or kitchen appliance. In real dollars, their cost has been dropping for decades. Computers are now affordable to any middle-class family. Memory gets cheaper every day.

Mass customization has made it possible to get more products just the way you like them. Convenience foods are so common, it's sometimes difficult to find just the raw ingredients if you want to cook at home. You would think that the consumer would be happy. He/she isn't.

Now that we have done all the easy things to eliminate high costs, consumers expect the roll to continue. They have agreed to accept less from the distribution system and shop at warehouse clubs where service is generally not poor, it's nonexistent. While consumers may be willing to accept less service, sometimes they continue to demand quality in the products they buy.

Now the tough part begins, selling the intangible difference that is represented by research and service. Consumers can't always recognize the difference of service. We don't mention it on the label although we should.

The Boomers continue to ripple through the economy influencing styles and social mores. But in spite of their tremendous impact, they aren't the be-all-end-all that the media would lead you to believe. Still, demographers project a rather startling change in the median age that cannot be ignored.

In 1983, the median age was a young 30.9 years. By 1993, it had climbed to an even 35. By 2000, we can expect it to rise even further. That will have a significant impact on how we serve our customers and who is still in the workforce to do the serving.

Older customers are even more quality-conscious. They are extremely security-minded. Recall the stories of old folks, who starved to death, yet had mattressfuls of money that they were afraid to spend. Older people buy the bulk of luxury travel, eat ice cream by the gallon and want service in addition to price. They have the money.

It will take smart marketers to earn their business.

Positively Outrageous Service is a matter of wrapping an experience around the service transaction. It will take sharp operators who do just that to succeed in the coming years.

By 2000, the number of households earning over $100,000 will double. The number earning over $50,000 will explode. That's the good news.

In other news, more than three-quarters of all households will have two wage earners, long on the bucks but short on time. Nearly 12 percent of 25-34 year-olds still live at home. And, if that isn't enough, 22 percent of the workforce expects to have to deal with elder care within the next three years. The so-called "sandwich" generation will be more than pressed for time, they'll be darned near squeezed to death.

That's good news for folks who have a plan to take the sale right into the home. It's good news for mail order if the field doesn't get overcrowded. But it spells d-i-s-a-s-t-e-r for merchants who can't make shopping "worth it."

In a few words...the money looks like it will be there. Getting it will be a job for the pros.

Tom Curley made one more prediction that I have been trying to avoid.

He said that the gap between the haves and the have-nots will continue to widen. I wish he hadn't said that. But he did.

The hospitality folks are claiming that by 2000, nearly one-fourth of the population will work in that industry. Hospitality doesn't always translate to "flippin' burgers" but too often it does. That unavoidably signals low wages and, as of this moment, few benefits. If that trend continues to develop as predicted, the gap will have to widen.

For most of us, it means only that we can continue to eat out and travel at reasonable prices. But for those who do not see hospitality as entry-level work, as most of it is, they had better work like the dickens to maintain a set of job skills that will carry them through the continous change that is on the horizon for business in the coming years.

THE FUTURE OF SERVICE

Speed is everything...almost. In the coming years, speed of service will be almost everything. Quality of the product will no longer be a competitive point of difference. The consumer will be aware of product quality and make a decision based on his or her needs.

Speed of delivery will be a competitive advantage. In fact, this is already so. If you have about the same product at about the same price but can deliver immediately instead of overnight, you have an advantage.

In the coming years, convenience will be a bigger and bigger issue. There are two reasons for this. First, the consumer will have even less time to shop as more and more families become two wage-earner families. There will be less time available.

The second driving force behind the rise in the importance of convenience is across the street...your competiton...and every other service provider whether or not they are in your industry. The reason this is so is that your customer is being trained each and every time he is involved in a business transaction.

If the dry cleaner gives same-day service and you sell garden tractors, you had better figure a way to get just as fast. That may be a bit of an exaggeration but not by much. For certain you will be compared to others in your industry and related industries.

The good news is that if service is generally poor in your industry and your service is up to mediocre, you're a hero!

If speed of delivery is important, time and place will be critical. The service provider who can and will deliver directly to the customer will have a definite advantage, possibly more important even than price and quality.

What can you do right away that could give your product a speed, time and place service advantage? Could you deliver directly to the customer immediately, twenty-four hours per day? If the answer is yes, are you doing it? Why not?

Of course, all of this applies to the hours that we are available to the customer. Try to call for software support on the weekend. Not easy. And the first vendor who offers twenty-four hour, seven-day support gets my future business. Look at the success of LL Bean. Call them anytime and they are ready to serve. Of course, they offer quality...and they aren't cheap.

What's the point? There is a trade-off between price, quality and convenience. Offer convenience and quality and price becomes less of an obstacle.

On a related issue, how could you make your schedule fit that of the customer? Hotels ask us to check in and check out on their schedule. Why not tell a guest that they can check in when they want to check in and out on their schedule? We have computers, we could schedule odd hour check in and out.

Theaters can hardly avoid scheduling start time but when was the last time you heard of them asking patrons when they would prefer to have the movie start? Instead, we start movies based on the ability to get as many showings into the day as possible.

Lenny's...no, that's Denny's, serves breakfast anytime. Try that at Mickey D's.

Before the sale, we are working on our time. After the sale, we work on customer time. What can you do today to speed service after the sale? Faster check out? Faster delivery? Faster test results? Faster! Faster!

PROSUMER

Today's consumer is no longer as passive as in the past. Today the customer is informed and often a very active participant in the service transaction. When the customer gets involved in his or her own service, some folks have taken to calling them "prosumers."

Take for example, the customer who decides to shop via computer on one of the on-line services such as CompuServe or Prodigy. They handle most of the details of their service entering size, color and shipping options. If the order is not right, who is at fault? The system? The consumer?

Actually, both. And it is when the consumer shares responsibility for the production of his own service that he becomes a prosumer.

The ultimate example has to be Hallmark's new kiosk operations where customers create their own greeting cards. Prosumers.

MODULAR CUSTOMERS

Despite clever attempts to define customers using techniques such as psycho-demographics and ZIP-code analysis, in truth, customers are much more likely to exhibit component personalities.

Yes, we can predict future consumer behavior based on previous purchase habits, but not precisely. All BMW owners do not purchase all of their fuel at the full-service island. And Lexus owners are just as likely to be found loading bales of bulk toilet paper from a warehouse club as they are to be found parked outside the Ritz-Carlton.

All this means is that your customer is not so likely to have a tag on him either and that the decision to purchase or pass will depend on a number of factors that may vary by the moment. It also means that as a group, consumers have learned to distinguish between the product and the distribution system.

Prosumers understand that by expecting less of the distribution system, they can get high quality products at lower prices. Commodity-type products will become more and more difficult to sell at premium prices. If you expect to sell a commodity product you had better have your costs under control because price will be the key factor...unless you can do something to wrap a service experience around the transaction that makes the customer say, "WOW!"

The customer is always asking this question, "Is it worth it?" The factors that enter the equation include price, quality and service.

The smart marketer will be increasingly concerned with making service tangible. Too much of what we do is unseen by the customer. If we intend to live by some code other than "discount," we'll have to get much better at giving substance to the service we sell.

CUSTOMER SHARE

Once we have customers, we must learn to do everything possible to keep them. The cost of acquisition is almost always greater than the cost of retention. And likewise, it costs less to sell a new product to an existing customer than to find new a customer for an old product. Smart marketers will be on constant lookout for opportunities to create and to sell new products to old customers.

Lexus tracks each and every car it sells. They know what maintenance the car has had and when. They can use this data to notify the customer when additional maintenance is due. More important, they can use this data to create an ongoing relationship. Lexus customers are designed to be customers for life because Lexus will never give them a reason to go anywhere else!

What can you do to make tangible your service?

What can you do to foster lifetime relationships with your customers?

THE WORLD IS AN OYSTER

Thirty minutes and they'll be hungry again. There is an old saw that Chinese food is good but not all that filling. Well, the Chinese market and that of a potpourri of other emerging, make that exploding, markets will be good for business and hopefully, a half-hour after the first sale, they'll be ready to buy again.

According to the U.S. Department of Commerce, the top ten, unranked, emerging markets are China, Indonesia, India, South Korea, Turkey, South Africa, Poland, Argentina, Brazil and Mexico. They're hungry for quality products and each has a huge, growing middle class capable of saying yes to those sharp enough to ask.

Even though the definition of middle class hardly matches the way we define middle class in the U.S., these and other countries have finally unleashed market forces and there are not millions, but billions ready to buy! Global communications, the force that felled the Iron Curtain and the Berlin Wall, showed the masses freedom that they were hungry to taste. Now it is showing them products that they are hungry to buy.

And what can we sell? America, of course! Our number two export, (military weapons is number one) is...go ahead, guess. Haven't a clue, do you ? It's entertainment. That's right, American culture goes overseas every day in the form of CDs, movies and television shows. The hottest products anywhere are American.

Entertainment sells more than an evening of fun. It sells people on the idea of American jeans, fast-food and sport shoes...but entertainment is the big item.

In Brazil, 70 percent of the songs on the radio are in English. U.S. films are 70 percent of the gate and American television is seen everywhere.

Two Bulgarians were touring South Fork Ranch near Dallas where the famous television series by the same name was shot. (Dallas is seen in 165 countries where it has been dubbed in 83 languages. Imagine that!)

Dallas is still in first-run in many of those countries, many of which are former Iron Curtain countries such as Bulgaria. As the two Bulgarians were touring the Dallas museum, they rounded the corner and were shocked to see a display from a season cliffhanger.

"JR! Shot?"

If you don't want to miss being the next Dallas in your industry, better think about how you might someday say, "billions and billions served..." and not be talking about Big Macs.

8

THE ORACLE SPEAKS

There are a number of methods for dealing with the future. The continuum runs from ignoring the future to shaping the future. My feeling is that if you are not at least looking toward the future, you have a better than even chance of being run over by it. A friend of mine was fond of saying, "Even if you are on the right track, you are likely to be run over if you are just standing still."

When the Greeks ran the world, or at least the part of the world they knew about, they often turned to the great Oracle of Delphi. Even then, smart folks knew that to know the future is to control the present. And the Greeks didn't want to leave anything to chance.

They spent a lot of time begging the Oracle to look into the future and share a tip or two that would guarantee success at the track. But the Oracle is dead so we'll have to turn to more conventional and, probably much more accurate, methods for our forecasts.

The simplest method for seeing into the future is to look at the trends of today. Yogi Berra, the great futurist and raconteur, said something to the effect, "You can see a lot just by looking." And there are plenty of professional lookers to help you see your future. John Naisbett, Edie Weiner and Marvin Cetron are such professional lookers. Rather than resort to the crystal ball, they use a more reliable technique...they watch the news. Lots of it.

By watching trade journals and literally counting the number of articles or mentions of a given topic, it doesn't require a sixth sense to discover hot trends well before they become "common knowledge." In fact, with the rapid change of pace today, by the time something becomes "common knowledge," it isn't.

Every few years, you can count on these futurists to publish a book detailing their analysis of the hottest, most influential trends. In between time, you can subscribe to their newsletters, which in addition to being good reading, are usually surprisingly useful.

How do you create your own, more product-industry-organization specific forecast? Simple. Ask the oracle and the oracle will speak.

There are several variations on a technique often referred to as the Oracle of Delphi. The simple steps are:

1. Ask a sample group to individually make predictions about expected trends, problems, or developments. Have them rank either or both the likelihood and/or impact of each possibility. Collect the data.
2. Combine and rank the data again. Redistribute.
3. Ask individuals to rank the predictions from the above report.
4. Collect and rank again to produce a final report.

It sounds much more complicated than it is and the results are almost always astounding in both foresight and insight. The technique takes advantage of the combined experience of the group. It tends to minimize preconceived notions and, because it is group work done individually, the anonymity allows ideas that may be controversial yet important to surface.

At a recent retreat that included executives from a wide cross section of America's finest corporations, we asked participants to look into the old crystal ball and predict the future for business and industry. Here's what they said (listed in order of probability):

1. Government regulations increasingly burden industry.
2. Information superhighway plays major role in the economy.
3. Consumers will demand high-touch balance to their high-tech lifestyles.
4. Communications will be constant and instant.
5. "Right-sizing" will continue.
6. Increasing illiteracy will make it more difficult to find qualified employees.
7. Soaring illegitimacy will turn employers into parents.
8. Aging boomers will continue to command the economy.
9. NAFTA and international trade will have a bigger impact on industry.

10. The work-at-home movement will spread.

In spite of the power of this simple exercise, it can be easily manipulated. More accurately, the participants can be easily manipulated. Simply presenting a list of future possibilities can easily shape the response of the participants. To obtain the above results, we presented the following list:

TRENDS

Soaring illegitimacy rate

Home shopping

The information superhighway

Work at home

Increased use of delivery services

Mass customization

Convenience foods

Disposable everything

Instant-constant communications

High-tech demanding a high-touch balance

Polarized buying habits

Aging Boomers and the boomlet

NAFTA

Decline of Communism

Retail theater

"Right-sizing"

Increasing drop-out rate

What really matters is that the list you offer to stimulate discussion is designed to do exactly that, stimulate not manipulate. You may wish to begin the process with a short brainstorming session with the goal of generating the largest possible list of potentialities in the shortest period of time, not worrying about quality of ideas, merely quantity.

The important thing is that no matter how you go about looking at the future, you must at least begin to look. The better captains of industry are not about to wait until the future jumps up and bites them on the backside. They are looking into the future. They are planning for the future. They are creating the future.

PART II

VALUES

1

AT THE FOUNDATION

"The purpose of mission, vision and ownership is to allow the organization to work leaner...call it enlightenment if you like, the result falls straight to the bottom line."

T. Scott Gross

Somehow in the midst of being politically correct we came to the false conclusion that in a diverse society the right thing, the polite thing, even the legally safe thing to do was to leave our personal values at home. Wrong!

Go ahead and look at the corporations that are doing really well. It's okay if you choose to use some measurement other than pure profitability. There is indeed more to life than the almighty greenback. Even if you wish to be pragmatic, at the heart of the best of the best, you will find a solid foundation of values, more often than not old-fashioned values, that ring of truth, justice and, as Superman would say, "The American Way."

Like it or not, every organization has a foundation of core values. As is true with the corporate personality, corporate values rarely amount to more than the aggregate sum of the personal values of everyone who is part of the enterprise. You may as well include suppliers, shareholders and even customers.

A corporate personality is the sum of individual personalities. The impact of a leader, who is strong and ever-positive, can still be nullified by a handful of entry-level staff who are just the opposite. The reverse is also true.

So it goes with corporate values. The corporate conscience is nothing more than the collective values of the entire crew. It matters little if the CEO is a person of strength and great character if the remainder of the roster reads like a Prison Times Who's Who.

Actually, the character of the leadership matters a great deal. Organizations inevitably reflect the character of their leadership. Michael Dukakis said it in the 1988 presidential campaign, "A fish rots from its head down."

Put a more optimistic face on it...the organization looks like the boss.

So it's a fair question to ask, "What is the character of the boss?" and "Does the boss bring conscience to work or check it at the door?"

This isn't to say that anyone should take advantage of a leadership position to proselytize. That would be downright unfair and in some cases illegal. But it is to say that managers have a responsibility to bring more than their brains to the office. They should also bring their hearts.

Do organizations that are led from the heart fare better than those that are led to the dollar? Fair question although difficult to answer.

(This chapter is being written at 30,000 feet on an orange Boeing 737 captained, at least figuratively, by a fellow named Herb Kelleher. Herb's Alfred E. Newman face is currently smiling from the cover of *Fortune* magazine, peering out from a headline that reads, "Is this America's Best CEO?" Stupid question...of course he is!)

Herb, and he doesn't do it alone, runs Southwest Airlines. Herb is one of the founders of this, the nation's sixth largest and only profitable, airline. It also may be America's most fun airline. No, it's probably the only fun airline. But then, that's Herb Kelleher, a man who seems to understand what Jim Miller so eloquently said, "When your job is fun, you never have to go to work."

Herb, and crew, have made Southwest Airlines a fun kind of place. At Southwest, fun is definitely a foundation value.

Every organization has foundation values; they just may be hidden.

How, or why, was your organization founded? To solve a problem? To give the founder an opportunity to be free from the heavy yoke of big business? To make money or make a difference?

And the biggest question may very well be, "Is the organization living up to those values, that original vision?"

No matter what were the original values or how noble they may have been, they are meaningless once forgotten. In the best of organizations, it is impossible to escape the foundation values. They are incorporated into nearly every part of corporate life.

In our little restaurant where we learned firsthand the value of values, we had a sign over the dining room door that simply read, "...don't forget to love one another." That unpretentious tag also closed out our radio commercials and frequently found its way to the bottom of employee memos.

It became my habit to verbally and visually remind the crew to love one another, most times when I would leave the store. Sometimes I would hold up two crossed fingers, (a little sign my grandmother taught me as her shorthand method for telling me that I was special.) Sometimes they would "salute" back, especially if they were too busy to talk. And that's how something as non-businesslike found its way into our "corporate culture."

TIME OUT FOR A STORY

We never were completely sure about this "love one another" stuff. Sure, it seemed to play well but there were times when as I left the restaurant and turned to remind the crew to love one another, well, I wasn't quite sure if they really bought into it.

One day a regular customer slid into a chair at my table while I wolfed a quick lunch. It was another of my short "bombing runs" to the restaurant. Sometimes I would run into the place just to show my support. This was especially common as our other businesses came to demand more and more of my time which inevitably meant that the restaurant would get the short end of the stick. After all, the place was running pretty smoothly and they really didn't need me as much as I needed to be needed, by what we always referred to as "the store", which meant in every sense of the world, our life savings — in fact, our life's efforts. (Does this sound familiar, anyone?)

So this customer, a regular, a woman for whom we could prepare lunch the instant we spotted her car, turn signal flashing "Church's," was crossing the bridge towards our place.

"May I join you?" she asked, after picking up her regular order.

"You already have. How's your day?"

"You know," she continued, ignoring my nothing of a question, "I've finally figured out why I like eating here."

This time she was inviting me to say, "Why?" so I did. "Why's that?"

"These people really love one another."

I made a joke about love being a necessity in such a small workspace but to tell you the truth, I was mighty glad that it was so darned noticeable.

A few months after we sold the joint, when I was still going through withdrawal, Melanie and I were sitting on the tailgate of our pickup, waiting for the local Christmas parade to find its way to us. A small truck pulled to a stop next to us. Out jumped a former employee, Dave Thomas. (Not the Dave Thomas of Wendy's fame but just as important to us.)

Dave appeared to be fiddling with something on the passenger side. In a few seconds he straightened up and turned to show us a small child.

"Hi, guys! I want you to see my son." Dave was as proud as proud can be. Naturally, we oohed and awwed as if he were holding the treasure he imagined. Fact of the matter is that we would have done the same thing had he been holding a Pekingese. Dave was sharing something personal and very, very important.

Before we knew it, Dave was back in the truck about to pull into traffic. But what he did next makes our point. Suddenly he stopped, rolled down the window and leaned out, fingers crossed in our "love one another" salute, saying, "Hey, guys. Don't forget to love one another."

I'm not saying that every organization should count love as a key foundation value, but it wouldn't hurt. Actually, it's sufficient to say that your foundation values don't all have to be lifted from an MBA curriculum.

At Southwest Airlines, those folks actually seem to love one another and it doesn't seem to be what you would call a problem. In fact, they were just named the number one, make that "the best", airline in the nation. Not bad for an organization where it's perfectly fine, actually encouraged to love one another — and the customers, too!

So how about your organization? Do you love one another? Heck...do you even **like** one another?

When we finally decided to organize the speaking and consulting business, we decided to do all the things we had done intuitively. Instead, this time, we'd actually do it on purpose. A plan of sorts, like we actually knew what we were doing. And why not? We were starting from scratch just like many of today's companies will have to do no matter what year the "Since ___" sign reads out front.

We gathered the troops and sat them down with nothing more than a few starter suggestions and the charge that we should build a company that would make us proud. Each of us had had experiences with organizations where the foundation values had long since been forgotten. Only this time, we were determined to operate on really important values and not let them be lost in the hurry towards growth and profit. Here are the five that we chose:

Intelligent risk

Customer first

Love one another

Ownership

Consensus management

Intelligent risk because we had all seen or been a part of organizations that had turned a corporate back on opportunity simply because it required a little risk. Usually organizations miss opportunities not so much from the fear of losing a few bucks but from fear of losing face if a failure is born from thinking out of the box. Well, to hell with the box and the risk and the potential for embarrassment. Look instead at the godawful pain brought on by a critical mass of "could-have-beens."

Customer first because it was the loving on the customer that had brought us to the party in the first place and we thought that might be a pretty good road on which to continue.

Notice, please, that we didn't say, "customers first." We felt like the future of service was pointed in the direction of mass customization where every customer gets exactly what she wants, exactly the way she wants it. So, for us, it's "customer first." One at a time — and we hoped there would be lots of them!

Love one another was, for us, another key choice. We had all been with organizations where more energy was spent either playing corporate politics (or defending against them) than was spent doing the things that really mattered. Besides, wouldn't it be nice to really enjoy the people on your team? Wouldn't it be great to know that everyone around you actually wanted to make you look good rather than be looking for an opportunity to advance at your expense? And wouldn't it be great to work with folks who you would be honored to have as a guest in your home?

We thought so and chose "love one another" to help remind us of those ideas as well as the fact that life is indeed short. Why not make the best of it?

Ownership was another important value. Why create an organization where a few get rich by keeping the majority poor? We believe that if we create an opportunity for everyone to be rewarded according to contribution, no one would be out looking for greener pastures. We wanted to create a place where it would truly be one-for-all and all-for-one. We're close but still not yet perfect. Still, it sure is nice to hear folks referring to the business as "my company."

Consensus management made our list and this one is a pure, no-nonsense business decision. Right up front we realized that the best way to keep office expenses to a minimum was to keep the office to a minimum. That either means no-growth or work-at-home.

You can't have at-home workers who feel no ownership and who need to be managed. So it was "kill all the managers" and hire only folks who could and would manage themselves.

We also had all felt the sting of autocratic management where good people rarely got better because they were never given a chance to fly on their own. That, we said, wouldn't happen to us.

So we created a real policy. All major decisions are made by a group that we call our peer council. And the vote must be unanimous. We feel that if an idea isn't strong enough to deserve the unreserved support of the entire group, we will be better off waiting for an idea that does.

A LITTLE CULTURE

The sum of your corporate values is your corporate culture. Period.

A consultant, who works with corporations on such issues as teamwork and culture, was approached by the CEO of one of her client companies. He said, "I've been hearing a lot about this corporate culture stuff and I was wondering, could you have one for us in time for a four o'clock meeting?"

She smiled and said, "Sir, I believe that you already have one."

And she was right. Like it or not, enlightened or downright medieval, your organization already has a culture. So before we go any further, try this exercise:

In 25 words or less, describe your corporate culture.

_____

_____

_____

_____

2

1, 2, 3...CULTURE!

By now, you may be ready for a little help. Since recreating a corporate culture is not an instant process, let's go back to those key, foundaton values. Have you thought about the ones that are most appropriate for you?

Oops! I should have said, "most appropriate for your organization." As long as the toothpaste is out of the tube, if your personal values are not in fairly close harmony to those of your organization, you better put this book on hold while you polish your resume. If there is one sure way to be miserable on the job, it has to be to work where your principles are horribly out of sync with those of the organization.

To help you begin the process of thinking about foundation values, here are a few suggestions...

Honesty	Trust	Fairplay	Casual
Family	Ownership	Consensus	Leadership
Teamwork	Sharing	Pride	Professionalism
Quality	Truth	Community	Open
Value	Freedom	Ethical	Old-fashioned
Low price	Integrity	Dependable	Excellence
Competitive	Responsible	Caring	People first
Innovation	Aggressive	Love	Customers first
Empowered	Flexibility	Passion	Intelligent risk

There! Now you have at least enough to get started. But the next question is..."How do I get started?"

Glad you asked.

You don't.

For a change in foundation values to take place, all of the key players must be represented if not included in the process. This means that a culture change is not something that can be decreed from corporate. Worse, ask the marketing department to whip up a jazzy new slogan, buy a ton of media time and tell the world about the "All New ABC Group," and stand by for disastrous results.

I can't tell you how many times in a former life we rolled out new programs only to find out that what worked great in the lab and tested well in focus groups was miserably executed in the field. Every time the problem was simply that there was zero buy-in from the folks who had to execute the plan on a daily basis. All we had accomplished with our scarce marketing budget was to run a few hundred-thousand new customers into our stores so that they too could see that we weren't ready.

To get serious about a corporate culture change, you must start at the beginning and include everyone who can make or break the process.

DISCOVERING FOUNDATION PRINCIPLES

While the trend is toward the "softer" values of ethical, human-centered business practices, a criminal enterprise would have as core values such as deception, theft and selfishness. (These aren't all that different from those practiced by many legitimate corporations!)

What are the values of your organization? How are they different from the values that you wish to promote? If political infighting and featherbedding are your current operating standards, better to list them and their rules for engagement. Simply filling in the blanks with warm fuzzy words won't have much, if any, impact on reality.

Guidelines

Limit to a few "core" values.

Keep them believable.

Corporate values are the personal values of the group.

Avoid proselytizing.

Example:

We believe that the organization should exemplify the values of this customer first, ownership, intelligent risk, and loving one another.

Foundation Value: _____

Management Philosophy: _____

_____

_____

THE BEGINNING

Now that we've brought it up, just where is the beginning?

A fine gentleman and CEO of a major international corporation read my first book, *Positively Outrageous Service,* and was very excited over the concept, deciding in the process that he would make his company a truly POS place to work and with which to do business. Nice thought.

He ended up calling my office in a near state of anger, frustrated over the undeniable fact that Positively Outrageous Service is much easier to talk about than to actually do. He had led the charge up the hill towards fun, customer-first service and was bewildered to discover that when he got to the top of the hill and turned to congratulate his troops...he was alone.

The problem was simple. Everyone had heard his call to POS but no one actually believed that: a) he really meant it; and b) it might make a difference for them.

He had failed to sell the concept. In fact, he had figured that since the idea was so very simple, so very attractive, so very obvious, the solution to the company ailments was that everyone with half a brain would not only follow him up the hill but probably beat him there. Wrong.

The beginning step is this:

Get everyone who has a stake in the process together and begin by asking them to clearly and candidly list the values that are currently shaping decision-making.

Be prepared for the brutal truth. You may need to encourage the process by using standard brainstorming techniques that promote getting as many ideas on the board as possible without taking time to argue or be judgmental. Then, if you wish, use the Delphi technique outlined in another chapter.

Since this first step can be a bit tough for some folks to swallow, give it time to settle in the minds of those who participated. Go back and ask if anyone would like to amend the results.

It may be that, once this far into the process, you may wish to stop. It's possible that although the results show your company to be far from an enlightened place to work and do business, it's just possible that for the personalities involved, including your customer base, things are just fine the way they are.

One good friend, who is the CEO of a major corporation, shared a somewhat unexpected outcome. As his company got deeper and deeper into its search to define corporate values and culture, it became apparent that not everyone was going to be comfortable with the results. One of the officers eventually stepped forward and tendered his resignation saying, "I agree with what you are trying to do. It's probably even the best thing for the company. But to tell you the truth, all of this customer first and empowerment stuff just isn't me."

Once you have and can deal with an accurate assessment of current corporate values, it's time to get to the fun part of the process; departing from reality long enough to begin thinking about how things would be in the best of all possible worlds.

It's time to begin thinking, perhaps for the first time intentionally, about what values you want to serve as the guiding principles of your company. Remember this must be a corporate effort that includes all of the stakeholders. The least productive approach would be to order up a corporate retreat, negotiate a few rope-and-obstacle courses and come home with a declaration to force-feed to the troops and hang on the lobby wall.

You'll find yourself with my friend, standing on the hilltop, pretty much alone.

THE PROCESS...

The process is uncomplicated although anything but simple. Here's the outline that we will be following...

Foundation Values...Management philosophy

Condition Statement

Key Market Trends

Mission Statement...Critical Success Factors

Vision Statement

Key Objectives...Short Term

Position Statement

3

SNAPSHOT!

WHAT CONDITION OUR CONDITION'S IN...

Before we can really get cooking on where we are going, we have to handle the issue of where the heck are we now, right now! Once you have articulated the foundation principles, sometimes called "core values," it's time to look closely at the current condition.

We call this process "snapshot!" Snapshot pretty well explains the exercise, describes the condition of the organization in a few words.

We want to...

> ➤ Mention organization history.
> ➤ Mention current strategy.
> ➤ Determine the current market and customer profile.
> ➤ Determine the products of the organization.
> ➤ Determine how the organization is structured.
> ➤ Determine the size and scope of the organization.
> ➤ Describe the environment in which the organization competes.
> ➤ Determine what it costs to acquire a new customer.
> ➤ Determine the value of a customer.
> ➤ Determine the retention rate of customers.
> ➤ Determine how much it costs to acquire and train a new employee.
> ➤ Determine what is currently being spent to upgrade current employees.

Example:

T. Scott Gross & Company, Inc., is a small organization founded by Scott and Melanie Gross.

It was primarily a family business for the first four years, concentrating on producing low-cost, vendor-funded video training programs and keynotes and seminars mostly on customer service.

When Scott published *Positively Outrageous Service*, the company was able to define a niche as customer service experts. Sales boomed as demand for speaking grew while a key account in the home center industry greatly increased sales on the video side.

Today, the company numbers about a dozen professionals working independently and in ad hoc groups on a project basis. Management is largely self–management although key decisions are made by a Peer Council, a group of five representing the major areas of endeavor; group events, keynote events, video production, administration/scheduling and product development.

The primary market is the hospitality/travel/entertainment industry and the targeted region is Texas.

SNAPSHOT! TAKE A SNAPSHOT OF YOUR ORGANIZATION.

_____

_____

_____

_____

_____

_____

_____

_____

_____

_____

_____

_____

KEY MARKET TRENDS...

There is little point in jumping ahead to creating mission statements until you first stop to think about where your enterprise may be heading if you continue on the current course. You may have one direction pretty well in focus but which way is the market heading?

Do you remember arguing over who would get up to change the television channel? If you do: a) you are old; and b) you should hope that your sole source of income is not the sale of channel selector knobs.

The point is that there is no point to creating a mission for an organization without a market. What will happen to many of the medical research
foundations if they ever find a cure? What will happen to the Post Office
when the information superhighway makes the first-class package a thing
of the past and Federal Express and UPS capture the last of the parcel
delivery business?

That's not a swipe at anyone, just a comment that the world is changing
and that if you and your organization intend to be there when it's over, you
had best begin to think beyond your mission. Mission has to be determined
with respect to the market. Otherwise, you are wasting your time.

Here is a list of questions that need to be explored...

➢ Why do people use our product?
➢ How could we make this product obsolete?
➢ Why do we market to this customer in this way?
➢ How is our customer likely to change?
➢ What would constitute breakthrough product or service?
➢ What is the reasonable lifespan of the product?
➢ What trends are forecast for our industry? What if they come true?
  What if they come earlier than expected?
➢ What other products are a natural for this organization?
➢ How would we answer the above questions concerning the
  individual internal processes in our organization?
➢ What is the life expectancy of our product?
➢ What position do we own or could we own?

Go ahead! Use your imagination to begin to explore. Play a good game
of "What if?"

➢ What if our supplier went out of business?
➢ What if our costs doubled overnight?
➢ What if our product went suddenly out of fashion or was linked to
  a disease?
➢ What if we invented a product to compete with one of ours?

Get the idea? All of the above "what ifs" have happened. Can you think
of the products or services that were involved? So, how come you haven't
played "What if?" with your own products and services?

There are some tricks to playing "What if?" that will make the process
more fun. Begin by dividing the process into three steps: List, Imagine,
Respond.

First, list everything you can imagine that could impact the situation. List every factor that could even remotely come into play such as people, organizations, things, events, even the weather.

Second, imagine how each factor or combination of factors would influence your organization if they actually occurred.

Third, dream up a response-scenario. Try not to let your natural inclination toward either optimism or pessimism shape your response ideas. It's best to try to think of both positive as well as negative outcomes for each of your scenarios.

Let's try an example...

Benowix manufactures air fresheners from a type of pine oil found only in the rain forests of Brazil. The oil that is used must be processed in the Benowix plant within four weeks of harvest or it turns rancid. Benowix has been able to charge premium prices due in part to clever marketing that promised that a portion of each sale would be set aside for the preservation of the forests.

List...

➤ Weather in the rain forests.

➤ Ability to import natural oils from Brazil.

➤ Containers for shipping.

➤ Shipping rates.

➤ Shipping speed.

➤ Consumer fascination with rain forests.

➤ Price stability.

➤ No known artificial substitute.

➤ Supply is available year-round.

Imagine...

➤ Public loses interest in rain forests.

➤ Brazil demands punitive higher export taxes in response to a U.S. embargo of Brazilian products due to non-cooperation on drug smuggling.

➤ Value of rain forest wood products soar due to spotted owl problems in the Pacific Northwest. This puts pressure to harvest entire tree.

➤ *60 Minutes* reports on the unsuspected health hazards of artificial air fresheners.

➤ A major competitor develops an inexpensive artificial substitute.

Responses...

➤ Go out of business.

➤ Look for an artificial substitute.

➤ Consider raising the source trees in south Florida.

➤ Purchase own rain forest acreage to guarantee supply.

➤ Support key members of Congressional Trade Committee.

➤ Diversify line and product type.

➤ Consider partnerships with others who promote rain forest products.

These are just a few things and ways that Benowix could list, imagine and respond to the hypothetical future. There are thousands of other trends that more generally influence the market and the future. We'll talk more about those trends in a coming chapter.

For now, this should give you the idea that the future can turn on a dime. The smart business leaders are always thinking about how such a turn, good, bad or indifferent, could impact sales, profits, even the whole face of the organization.

There is simply no point in creating that mission statement without at least thinking about what the future may look like without your influence. When you have given yourself permission to list, imagine and dream up a possible response, you are ready to begin thinking about how you might go about actually shaping the future.

4

Mission Statement

The Mission Statement defines the purpose of the organization. It should be written to serve as an internal slogan of purpose, a common goal serving as a center of focus.

CRITERIA

Short...easy to remember.
In Your Face...always top of mind.
Incorporates founding principles.
May incorporate key strategy.
Mentions the product and the targeted customer.
Mentions the uniqueness of the organization.

Examples:
"Protect and serve."
"Provide affordable family-style entertainment to visitors to Florida."
"Produce world-class transportation options for the discriminating consumer."
"Teach American businesses how to provide Positively Outrageous Customer Service."

Some organizations begin the foundation steps by creating the mission statement. We think that is okay but not the best approach. When the mission statement comes first, the values by necessity must come later. Others call the foundation values the "Critical Success Factors." It may be a matter of six of one...but we don't think so. We believe that you should start with your values, take a stand, tell us who you are or at least want to be, and then tell us why the organization was founded.

Whatever you do, draw your line in the sand sometime, somewhere.

Some values-driven organizations even opt to list critical success factors in addition to their foundation values. They look at these factors to be, not supplementary, but explanatory.

Our friends at Holt Companies in San Antonio, Texas, have put ethical business practices ahead of all. Not only have they decided upon a list of five core or foundation values, they have an additional list of values to guide the organization and another, corresponding list to shape corporate practices.

I CAN SEE CLEARLY...THE VISION

If the mission statement is a statement of purpose, the vision statement is a picture of purpose fulfilled. The vison statement describes the desired future in clear terms, providing focus to the mission.

The vision statement could look like...

- ➤ We will be number one in name recognition in chemically applied surfaces.
- ➤ We will be the largest purveyor of Italian specialty products in the southwest.
- ➤ Our graduates will be represented in the leadership of a majority of Fortune 500 companies.
- ➤ We will be the world leader in hair technology.

It is perfectly fine to let loose with a little optimism when you are writing the vision statement. Aim high but not so high that your vision is out of the realm of possibility. What you may not realize is exactly how much really is possible.

Marcia Wieder, author of *Making Your Dreams Come True*, had a modest goal. She wanted to become, we'll use the word "famous," but she may be a bit more modest, as she set out to become known as the leading expert in helping people realize their dreams. Of course, helping others realize their dreams would be the realization of hers.

How do you become famous? Well, you would know if you had seen Marcia on Oprah, Montel Williams and most of the other national talk shows. Get the point? Even if you are a four-foot-something dynamo from San Francisco, you can make your dreams come true...but not unless you dream them first!

Begin by sitting down with the folks you trust and dreaming about what is or could be possible. Colonel Sanders didn't make his mark until a time in his life when most men are winding down. The same is true for Ray Kroc and a host of other winners. So go ahead! Create a vision and don't be stingy with yourself. You may aim too high and miss. Worse, you could aim too low and hit.

GOAL CARD SERVICE...

Goals...Objectives...Strategies.

To clear the distinction, the mission statement is not a goal statement. The mission statement answers the question, "Why was this organization formed?" And the vision statement answers, "How do we want the future to look?"

The goal statement answers a related but still different question, "How will we know when we have achieved our mission and vision?"

Goals should be written, not just for the overall organization but for individual departments and sections. A general rule is that goals should be written at the level of execution.

Effective goals are...

Short

In your face

Tied to the mission

Too many organizations create goals that read like *War and Peace*, too long and cumbersome for mortals to remember or repeat let alone internalize. Human beings need goals that they can get their arms around.

"Uncle Sam Needs You" was a great slogan because it was all normal people needed as both a summary of the situation and a call to action.

And call people to action is exactly what an effective goal statement must do.

At Ford, quality is...

You instinctively filled in the blanks, didn't you? You knew that at Ford, Quality is Job 1.

If you know Ford's goal statement, how come you don't know yours?

Because either you don't have one, the greatest possibility, or you have one but it's too awkward to remember. Most folks when asked their company mission, vision and goal statements, just smile at you like a tree full of owls or, if they actually have an answer, they must rummage through their wallet to find the little laminated card that the consultant left with them. (We do that, too, just in case you assumed that we actually had earned the right to cast the first stone.)

Objectives are...the little things that you do every day to get you closer to your goals. We like to say that objectives are the things that you do on a daily basis that make the place better than it was then when you got there. And, if things aren't better when you leave, why did you show up at all? Do us all a favor and stay home!

There should be performance objectives set at, not for, all levels. And everyone should be required to have a current list of objectives for the day, the week and the near term. More about this later.

Strategies are quite another animal. Strategies are the little plans, the conduct required to achieve the goals. Strategies are such things as....

Quality guarantee.

Win the Baldrige Award.

Participate in industry organizations.

Hire the top talent in our industry.

Create a world-class retail space.

Look at them all this way...strategy is how we conduct ourselves and our business to enable us to achieve our objectives which are smaller goals that must be achieved on the way to our larger goal. Our goals help us realize our mission, our reason for existence. Our vision is our dream of how the world will look when we have achieved our mission.

POSITION IS EVERYTHING

If you can only read one marketing book, read Reiss and Trout's work, *Twenty-two Immutable Laws of Marketing*.

If you can only absorb one bit of wisdom, here it is...

"It's the marketing."

Whatever you do, there is nothing as important as the marketing. Having a great product is nice, maybe even very important. But it means nothing if people don't know about it, the advertising, and have great feelings about it...the marketing. Consumers don't always know why they buy one product rather than another. I do.

The products we buy are those that we feel good about.

Now you know.

Demming says that, "Organizations are designed to serve the customer."

I'll buy that. But they are also designed to create new customers and that doesn't happen easily, unless the customers they already have, are made to feel so good that they are compelled to tell others.

What this is leading to is the need to know up front what position you want to occupy in the mind of the consumer. Because if you don't know what position you want, how will you know what position to ask for? How will you know what position you want to create for yourself?

Determine core values first; you have to live with and by them. Then decide for what overall purpose you are dedicating your efforts. Work through the entire process. Whatever you do, don't stop short of the positioning statement. In fact, if you have little time or patience for the entire process, at least create your positioning statement and make certain that everything that you do works toward making that statement reality.

"America's Positively Outrageous Service Expert"

"World Famous Mexican Foods"

"The Wuerst Barbeque in Texas"

"Quality Automobiles for Families"

BILLBOARD!

When we visited Juanell Teague in Dallas, Texas, we had few if any expectations other than that she would have ideas to help improve our business. I expected to be visiting with a speaking coach who would share her brutal insights regarding technique. (Juanell is the recognized expert in the speaking industry, probably the only reason I would subject a sensitive ego to criticism.)

What we expected and what we got were two entirely different things.

The best part of the visit wasn't the visit at all. The best part arrived in the mail shortly after a long phone conversation that began with her encouraging me to make a commitment to my career and ended with an agreement to meet in Dallas within the month. She mentioned that she would be sending a package of materials that we should work on prior to traveling to Dallas. Since Melanie and I are a team, and since she seems to thrive on rules, paper and details, I passed this off as something that she would most likely handle.

When we opened the large envelope, our first thought was that you have to kill a lot of trees to work with Juanell. She had sent enough paper to require an environmental impact statement. Al Gore should use Juanell's paperchase as a warm up before he gets too far into his project to reinvent government. There were forms for the forms.

"What does this have to do with being a better speaker or consultant?" I choked.

There, buried in the middle of pages that asked me to list target industry contacts and requests for presentation bullet points, was the most important document of all. One plain page with little print and too much white space. It simply asked me to write in six words or less who I was and what I did.

I couldn't do it.

I had spent years building a repertoire of presentations that could qualify me to speak to any group on any occasion. Now this wild woman, who clearly knew nothing about speaking or consulting or whatever, had the gall to ask me to limit myself to six or fewer paltry words!

I decided to humor her.

At first I wrote funny descriptions. "Jack of all trades." There. That's only four words. But it does rather beg the reader to complete the cliche.

There was "The Cheaper Speaker." Nice rhyme but it invites the thought that perhaps there might be a quality issue.

We tried a dozen or so six-word combinations. Bear in mind that this was before Positively Outrageous Service had finally brought function to form. Speaking was the dream. It didn't seem all that important to actually settle on a topic! I thought a microphone and a silver tongue was what attracted clients! How was I to know that people wouldn't want to fly me halfway around the world to speak to them on a topic that could be ably delivered by most any junior college instructor?

Then I got it. Juanell was asking me to stand out. And while being outstanding would be an admirable accomplishment, it was standing out that made the difference!

Before I could become successful, I would have to tell people in a busy world just why they should stop long enough to decide if I was the one they wanted. And that just wouldn't happen unless I could, in six words or less, arrest their attention and tell them exactly what it was that made me special. Exactly who I was and what I could do for them.

"America's Positively Outrageous Service Training Expert!"

Six fat, juicy words that said in a heartbeat what I did, where I did it and even why I should be your choice.

You could argue that there may very well be even better ways to articulate the product and service. In fact, if you have a better idea, send it along. Thomas Watson of IBM fame once said that to be successful, a company had to be absolutely willing to change the things it did and the way it did them as long as it remained forever committed to the principles that defined its corporate soul.

So send me your six words or fewer billboard...but only after you have created a really hot one for yourself.

Incidentally, that was no typo. You really should create a six words or fewer personal billboard. It really puts things in perspective as you go about the simple business of living life. And you never know when you will find yourself sitting in front of a potential employer who has the treasure of Caesar but lacks the patience of Job.

"Tell us in six or fewer words exactly who you are and what you do. Make us take notice and the job is yours."

KEEP ON TRUCKIN'

Another word for your six-words billboard is "slogan." Here are a few ideas, lifted from the telephone book just to get you started:

Smart Mail Business Mail Center — (This is also the name of the business!)

We love to fly, and it shows — (Delta has a mission and billboard combined!)

When it absolutely has to get there overnight — (Federal Express cheated by a few words but we'll let 'em slide.)

A+ Energy Management, Air Conditioning, Heating — "You can't do it better than A+" — (That's their official slogan)

Truck Collision Specialists — (Any questions?)

Quick Lube. America's 10-Minute Professionals — (Nice!)

Ready-mixed Concrete for all Purposes — (Not glamorous but it works)

La Quinta...Just right, overnight! — (Says it all!)

Circuit City, where service is state of the art — (Lots of message in this one)

And here are a few that don't work:

Keeping Austin Totally Satisfied — (What kind of business is this?)

Feeding the world on the go — (Sounds dangerous to your health)

No Job Too Small — (But are some too large?)

Nation's Oldest — (Good thing they're not the world's oldest)

POINT?

If you can't say who you are and what you do in about six words, how can you tell your employees what is to be the absolute focus of their efforts?

Whether you run a major corporation, a small business, a single department or that mini-corporation yourself, it's a modern-day imperative to have your billboard up and ready. Ready to tell the next customer what it is that makes you stand out. Ready to remind yourself to keep on target.

One other thing I keep hearing from Juanell would serve you well, too. She keeps reminding her clients to, "Focus — or die."

5

CULTURE

Creating the Plan

➤ Seven foundation steps
➤ Short-term plans
➤ Individual plans by department and individual
➤ Building in the reward
➤ Measuring results
➤ Creating feedback and reinforcement

I'D RATHER FIGHT THAN...

Old enough to fill in the blanks? If you are, you'd rather fight than switch. And, if you are like most people, you'd rather fight than change. Actually, people don't resist change as much as they resist being changed. Your job as a leader is to create an atmosphere where change is a natural, comfortable way of doing business.

The above reads well but in real life, it is harder than the dickens to make happen. Why? Fear is the simple explanation. The larger version is to point out that (particularly if the organization is or has recently been successful), managers are naturally led to believe that whatever were the conditions that led to the original success are just what the doctor ordered to insure success in the future.

It's the old story of dancing with whomever brought you to the party in the first place.

Organizations are bundles of activities. We create boundaries around those activities in the form of policies and procedures that allow them to be managed, call it controlled. When the activities have been successful, we are reluctant to change the policies and procedures that hold them in place. We invest heavily in terms of money, bureaucracies and traditions to make certain that the goose that laid the original golden egg doesn't get away. We know what works and do everything possible to keep it working.

Success is a two-sided coin. On the one side lies market conditions. On the other is the response of the organization. If the relationship is successful, then the organization is wise to erect barriers to change but only as long as the market dynamic remains static.

Where we get into trouble is when the market changes and the forces inside the organization continue to hold in place behaviors that remain targeted on a market that no longer exists. The organization is afraid to tamper with the multi-layers of defenses that had been created to the organization from itself. The defenses become the problem and the entire organization drifts into denial, afraid to admit that the world has changed and that old practices no longer work.

Ford is a great example of reluctance to change. They had been very successful in the early days and, like other organizations, had created enormous bureaucracies and systems to ensure that success would continue. It wasn't until nearly too late that they finally recognized the writing on the wall.

Said Ford Chairman Donald Peterson, "A large corporation will keep doing what it does as long as profits hold out...we didn't listen to our customers until the message was written in big, big numbers." (Like billions.)

There are plenty of reasons why change is not readily embraced. Change is not a neat, orderly process. It is often upsetting and very, very messy. It requires sacrifice, often human.

Here are just a few of the reasons why folks resist change...

Fear of...

> ➤ Loss of control. (Compensation and status is often based on a manager's control over people and resources. Change often threatens loss of that control.)
> ➤ Surprises. (People like surprises...good ones. But they are afraid of the unknown. If we could predict the future, change would be easy.)
> ➤ Cost of confusion. (There are genuine costs associated with the confusion that often accompanies change. They have to be considered, even budgeted.)
> ➤ Loss of face. (If you have been fighting change, you have to

hold your position even after you have been convinced.)

➤ Concerns about competence. (Change may require new mastery. Can an old dog learn the new tricks?)

➤ More work. (People who have fallen into a comfortable routine, don't often go looking for challenge...it's hard work!)

➤ Ripple effects. (While some change may be tolerated, what happens if we open the floodgate to more?)

➤ Past resentments. (Change that is perceived to reward rivals will be resisted...it may not be right but that's life in the big organization!)

➤ Genuine threat. (Sometimes change really does threaten...usually those who have reason to worry.)

ABOUT CHANGE...

The law of entropy argues against most of what we do in human organization. Organizations, at least those of the industrial age where change occurred at a relatively slow pace, are designed around the preservation of the status quo. Organizations have been, by their nature, paranoid, always looking for ways to protect assets, often ignoring opportunities that would have required intelligent risk. That has to change.

There are three areas of change: Marketing, organizational and political. And one does not change independently of the other. Too often, the marketing department gets out in front of the organization making promises that the organization simply cannot keep. There is an explanation but no excuse.

The marketing folks are generally charged with listening to customers. When customers speak, the marketing department responds by making the promise that the market wants to hear. Too bad. Marketing is in the business only of making promises.

Operations keeps promises, or should. Making promises is the easiest job. Operational or organizational change has to consider political change, too. There is little point in attempting to change a corporate culture without considering the political implications. Whose territory could be threatened? Whose competency could come into question? Who has a management style that simply has to go?

Can we avoid change? Absolutely! At least for awhile. Joel Barker, author of *Paradigms*, says that if you want to keep your paradigm, (your way of viewing and hence doing business), all you have to do is change your customer. Or, it may be that you would want to change your paradigm and keep the customer.

Trust me, if you intend to hold onto the old ways forever, eventually your customers are going to die and you'll have to either die with them or spend a lot of effort looking for more.

Barker says that you manage within paradigms and lead between them. The problem has been that, in an era when change does not come at a rapid pace, management that is simply good at holding on can be pretty darned successful. It's only when change begins to break over you like a wave on a stormy beach that management must give way to leadership. And when major change becomes more than something that we deal with every decade or so and we begin to face potentially crushing change on a constant basis, then the idea that a manager is all it takes to run a vital organization is a very dead idea indeed.

The idea of keeping up with the competition is also a recipe for disaster.

"Doing the same thing as your competitors is the risk. If they fail, you fail."

Kenji Asao, **Wall Street Journal 4/94**

Need more evidence? Even the army is beginning to realize that they must begin to look at the world in a different light. Recently they have begun looking at how to increase "lethality, tempo and survivability" on the battlefield. Lethality, tempo and survivability. Does that describe the world of business today or what?

Lethality. Not meeting competition but beating them to the punch. Lethality. Not merely producing a quality product but producing quality that sets the standard.

Tempo. The organization of today and tomorrow must be built around change and dissent must not be tolerated; it must be cultivated. Tempo. The organization of today and tomorrow will master the ability to anticipate rather than respond.

Survivability. Not being content to win the market today but anticipating the market of tomorrow. Survivability. Not creating the best management team but creating the best team of self-managers.

The organization of tomorrow, the one that leads rather than hangs on, will be a dynamic organization where teams will form and fade, solve problem sets and then dissolve. Tomorrow's teams will be fluid as will the organization chart.

If we haven't been describing your company, you are due to change.

CREATING CHANGE...

Change strategists. Change implementors. Change recipients. Those who decide. Those who do. And those whose job is not to question why. Theirs is but to do or die. Nonsense!

There should be no dividing up in a culture change process. Everyone involved with any phase should be involved in every phase. That's how you create change, by starting from the inside out rather than from the top to the bottom.

DON'T SELL ME...

Team players don't want to be sold much more than they want to be told. They want to be asked. The true masters of change recognize that the basis of fear is the unknown. They include as many of the stakeholders as possible in the change process and those that are not directly involved are at least directly informed.

Still, not everyone will be a willing player. It is said that Lee Iaccoca had a project to develop a minivan while he was at Ford but made little progress because he felt that he had to keep it hidden from Henry Ford.

In a former life, we often worked in semi-secrecy to bring projects through development before they could be killed unceremoniously without trial by our conservative "management". Regardless of the culture you would like to develop, you must learn to work with the culture that you already have. Begin by thinking about the cultural forces that are already at play.

Is your organization highly political? Why? Who or what holds that in place?

Is your organization highly traditional? What traditions could be beneficial? Harmful?

Who are the formal and informal leaders? What are their needs?

Who are the stakeholders? Customers? Vendors? Shareholders? Competitors?

How would you describe your organizational culture? You need to know before you undertake to change its culture. It may be easier to go play on another team. Do you hear that? It may be easier and a whole lot less risky to just find yourself somewhere else to play.

Mark Sanborn, author of *TeamBuilt*, suggests a quick analysis...

Which best describes the situation...

Attribute (0)	score 0-10	Attribute (10)
Competes with each other	____	Challenges the competition
Personal agenda	____	Team agenda
Conservative	____	Innovative
Requires kick-start	____	Self-starters
No personal linkage	____	Linked to team success
Independent	____	Overly dependent
Tolerates others	____	Enjoys each other
Little urgency	____	Sense of urgency
Resists challenge	____	Responds to challenge

Whatever you do, before attacking sacred cows, it is wise to remember that things got this way for a reason, not by accident. Which means that any cow could be sacred. Plus, even if the cow you intend to roast doesn't belong to anybody in particular, it is the property of the system. That means that in addition to the emotional baggage that comes strapped to sacred cows, there is at least some investment in systems, policies and procedures that had been made to hold things in place. So any move should be considered an attack.

When you go on attack, don't go alone and don't attack from the front or attempt to win the battle in a single charge. That's a certain formula for defeat, especially if you meet unexpected resistance. Instead, win friends for change one player at a time. In the long run, changing the organization one soul at a time actually takes less time and a whole lot less effort than attempting to change everything at once.

There are three simple steps to changing an organization:

Change one person at a time.

Be patient until you build "critical mass."

Change yourself first.

As you begin the process, look for examples that might serve as a model. Why reinvent the wheel? Don't limit your search for examples to your industry. Remember, if your industry is backwards, you could find yourself imitating the best of the worst.

Look for the best example you can find...anywhere. While you are at it, ask someone to serve as your mentor. You can discover the pitfalls without falling or at least without falls that are fatal.

ASKING...INVOLVING...

Many of our clients have asked about corporate retreats where the issues of culture could be addressed without interruption. Constructive interruption is exactly what the doctor orders! You need the constructive interruption of lots of little meetings where ordinary folks can be filled in and consulted on the process.

Jack Welch of General Electric is famous for his efforts to fully harness the energy of his energy giant. Probably the three best-known of his activities are:

Workout sessions

Best practices

Process mapping

WORKOUT...

Workout sessions, the way we see them, are great opportunities to challenge leadership to defend current practices and respond to team player suggestions. The rules should be simple. Any question, politely asked, is a good question. Every good question gets an immediate response or the promise of a response within a specified time.

Every suggestion must likewise get an immediate response ranging from instant approval to the formation of a committee to study the suggestion and report at a specified time.

If a spirit of openness, mutual respect and cooperation is part of the culture you want to promote, there may be no better way to demonstrate to the rank and file your commitment.

BEST PRACTICES...

Maybe it was Jack Welch or maybe it was Stew Leonard who elevated the idea of best practices to a fine art. Whomever is to be credited, companies that are willing to look anywhere in their search for excellence to be duplicated, enjoy a definite advantage over those who follow the practice of ignoring ideas that carry the "not invented here" label.

Best practices allow companies to consider adaptable ideas that come from any source.

Smart companies, looking to leverage change instead of fight it, should make the study of trends and the search for best practices the subject of regular brainstorming sessions. Each idea that shows merit should be assigned a champion whose task it is to gather more data and even give the most promising ideas a try.

PROCESS MAPPING

We'll save a full discussion of process mapping for later. Process mapping is a method of analyzing how work is organized. Making a cultural change always involves changing how work is organized. It always steps on toes and ruffles feathers. The gift of process mapping is that not only is it a great tool for making work flow more efficiently, often by eliminating unnecessary steps, but also that the solutions it presents are so objective that no one could argue that the recommendations are politically motivated.

Process mapping is useful for its let-the-chips-fall-where-they-may-objectivity.

GETTING TO CONSENSUS...MAKING THE CHANGE

Getting to consensus is often a matter of playing to concerns. Smart leaders don't wait for concerns to surface, they solicit them. Ask questions such as....

➤ In your opinion, what is the biggest barrier that we face?
➤ What do you think could make this process move faster or smoother?
➤ How do you think the others feel about the changes we are talking about?

Whatever you do, don't try to make huge changes overnight. Establish a timeline that is mutually agreed upon and do things in a gradual, step-by-step fashion.

Part of the cultural change process should include a marketing effort to put and keep the values top of mind. First, do this for internal consumption only. Don't make a plan to tell the world about your new service quality culture until it has already become such a part of the organization on the inside that customers are noticing and commenting from the outside. Then it is okay to let the rest of the world know. You will be telling them how things are — not how they are hoped to be.

CHANGING, STILL...

The secret to changing an organizational culture is as simple as ABC...Always Be Changing. When an organization accepts change as a way of life, as a way of doing business, it develops a certain resiliency that almost creates a sense of anxiety when things do not change for a while.

Rubbermaid may be the world's premier example of an organization built around and for change. They have as a goal to create and develop an average of one new product......every day.

Such momentum requires an organization that absolutely thrives on change yet is firmly rooted in its core values. It is not possible or healthy for an organization to be in constant turmoil. Only the mentally unbalanced can operate in a world where everything changes and nothing is the same. In the successful, dynamic organizations of tomorrow, almost everything can change but something must stay the same, the values.

And that is the hallmark of the successful organization of tomorrow...breaking the rules while honoring the values.

Evaluation

Present...where are you right now?

_____

_____

Future...what do you want to be when you grow up?

_____

_____

On what basis did you make the above decision?

_____

_____

Dreaming the dream

Who gets to help build the dream?
Customers? Suppliers? Internal customers?

_____

How do we get from where we are to where we want to be?
What financial resources may be required? Can we make that kind of commitment? Are the funds available?

_____

_____

What human resources will be required? Do we have them? Can we get them?

_____

_____

What sacrifices will be required? Are we willing to make the sacrifices, including losing current team players?

_____

_____

How do we sell the dream?

_____

_____

PART III

CUSTOMER EYES

1

SURVEY SAYS

When I needed to know for certain what American consumers think about customer service, I asked my friends at La Quinta Inns for a little help. They were in the middle of a new image campaign and I figured that they, too, would be interested in discovering how they fit into the mosaic of hospitality offerings. Was the new image really compatible with the expectations of their target market? Would the new, brighter look be perceived as an added value?

Together, we created a survey that would answer their questions and mine as well.

And the survey said...

FOR BETTER OR WORSE...

There's something intriguing about trends. We always want to know if things are getting better or growing worse. When times are bad, they don't seem quite so awful if there is at least some evidence that they are getting better. When times are good, we seem to need assurance that they are not getting worse. So we asked.

Are you satisfied with the service that you get at restaurants, hotels, department stores, airlines and utility companies?

Very satisfied	26%
Fairly satisfied	51%
Only somewhat satisfied	18%
Not at all satisfied	3%
Not sure	2%

(These last respondents have been living on another planet and cannot be expected to know how they feel about customer service.)

Overall, how do you think the level of service that you get today compares with customer service one to two years ago?

Getting better	18%
Getting worse	20%
Staying the same	61%
Not sure	1%

(Here you have a fairly even split among those who think that service is getting better and those who think just the opposite while the majority think there has been little change. Now watch what happens with the next question.)

Do you think that the level of service is better or worse compared to ten years ago?

Getting better	34%
Getting worse	36%
Staying the same	23%
Not sure	7%

(Again, respondents are about evenly split between those who see an improvement and those who think just the opposite.)

So, how do you interpret these results? I think they indicate that: a) Customer service is really pretty good; and b) It's probably getting better although the customer doesn't notice. That is probably due to the fact that over the past decade, American businesses have raised the bar, and along with it, customer's expectations of what it is that constitutes really good service.

Some folks, of course, argue that service is worse than ever and that the only reason it doesn't show in the polls is that consumers are now expecting even less. Well, I don't think so.

Compare customer service in the United States with service anywhere else in the world and I think you will agree that we are the world's service leaders. Great customer service seems to be a moving target. What was good service in the mid-80s is in many cases expected in the mid-90s. The hotel industry is probably the premier example of improved customer service.

Do you remember when there was no such thing as a "no smoking" room? Do you remember when check out meant a long line at the front desk in the morning? Do you remember when you didn't want to trust the hotel for your wake-up call, the only alternative was a "traveler's alarm clock?"

Today, non-smoking rooms are the rule along with video check out and in-room clock radios (although these are sometimes glued to the night table and facing away from the bed so that the only way you can tell if it's time to get out of bed is to get out of bed!)

SOME THINGS NEVER...

You probably filled in the blank on the previous header without even being aware that you did it. Some things never change. That's probably true about customer service because customer service is all about human nature.

When we asked 600 people what was the most important thing to them about customer service, almost everyone responded with a variation of the same answer:

Courtesy	49%
Friendliness	11%
Promptness	9%
Listen to you	7%
Knowledgeable	6%
Other	14%
Not sure	4%

Take the top four responses, add them together, divide by four, add your age and multiply by 2.338 and see if that's your house number. Better yet, add them together and discover that for at least 76 percent of the population, friendly customer service is more important than anything else. Think about it. There isn't much difference between courteous service and plain, ole friendly service. And isn't being respectful of someone's time by giving prompt service just another brand of "friendly?" Doesn't the same apply to listening to the customer? I think so.

I'll bet a hundred bucks that the "other" category also included a fistful of responses that could be interpreted as "friendly."

There's a lesson here that we'll look at closer in later chapters.

PLANES, TRAINS AND AUTOMOBILES

We just couldn't resist asking our version of the fabled "mirror, mirror, on the wall..." question. And, boy! Did we get a surprise or two!

We asked folks to tell us about service in a variety of industries and here's what they said:

	Excellent	Good	Only fair	Poor
Restaurants	11	61	24	3
Hotels	16	60	22	2
Department stores	6	57	32	5
Airlines	14	53	26	5
Car repair shops	12	37	33	18
Gas or electric co.	15	61	17	6
Local telephone co.	21	60	16	3
Local bank	31	51	13	4
Insurance companies	12	44	28	15
Discount stores	10	54	30	5

Lots of interesting things here!

First surprise...people are pretty happy with utility service. Not to take away from what must be a fine job serving the rate payers, but notice please that this is old, well-developed technology and there are very few opportunities to interface with utility providers. How often does your power go out? And when it does, how long does it stay out and do you even have to call in to complain? The same is true for the telephone. In this country, we flip on a light switch and expect there to be light. We pick up the phone and 99.999999 percent of the time, *voila*! A dial tone. When it comes to utilities in the the U.S., we're just plain spoiled.

That's almost as true for restaurants and hotels. Look at the number of respondents, who reported that they think service in these two industries is excellent or good, and you get an amazing 62 percent for restaurants and 66 percent for hotels! What does that mean if you are in either of these two industries? You had better be good because, according to our survey, your competition is.

Nearly one in five respondents reported that service is only fair. Who could afford to lose one in five customers and still survive? (The fact is more likely to be that the 22-24 percent who reported that service is "only fair" are not likely to be customers of the top tier providers...yet. **And**, what constitutes the so-called "top tier" is increasingly not the same as the top tier in terms of price. Get it? The so-called "little guy" is learning fast!)

Car repair shops did poorly probably for two reasons. First, it's a major pain in the ya-ha to be without your car. So the nature of the beast almost forces the scores lower.

Or does it? It could also be said that where there is more opportunity for customer inconvenience, there is also more opportunity to surprise and delight customers who really aren't accustomed to getting happy service from you or your competition.

The second reason that auto repair faired so poorly is probably just plain, old, poor service. This is an industry that continues to be dominated by folks who just love cars. That's what turned them on as a kid. That's what continues to turn them on when they go into business. Maybe the survey is hinting that the key to survival is to let the folks who love cars, work on them but turn the hard work of customer service over to someone, who thinks that customer service is a career rather than a distraction. That was not a swipe at the auto industry; it was a suggestion that just might make a difference.

The real surprise I've saved for last.

Add the top two scores for department stores and big box discounters. What do you get? Darned near the same number! You get 63 percent and 64 percent respectively. Hardly enough to say there is a difference.

The question is, do discounters score so well because they really give great service or is their score the result of lowered expectations? Visit a department store and try to find someone to help you. Repeat the experiment at a discount house and decide for yourself.

Just this morning a local columnist seemed to take great pleasure in ripping apart a locally-owned discounter after he had an absolutely terrible experience. Is there no hope of competing in the area of service if you are a large operation? Or are there tricks that can make service a competitive edge regardless of the number of folks on the payroll?

The answer is...any organization can give consistently great customer service. However, the smaller operation has the advantage, whether or not the ownership grabs it.

GETTING IT

From the beginning, folks have asked me not just how to give Positively Outrageous Service, but how to get it as well. So we asked our survey group what strategies they employed to get what they want when the service shoe is on the other foot. (No wonder customer service sometimes seems to be such an elusive commodity. People have no idea about how to get it!)

Asked how much influence they had over the quality of service they receive, customers had these pitiful responses to offer...

A lot of influence	12%
Moderate influence	48%
A little	24%
None	12%
Don't know	4%

Compounding the problem, customers are a pretty confused group when it comes to the price-value relationship between the price they pay and the service they get. We thought we were pretty smart to ask if the customer would be willing to pay more for some things if that guaranteed getting better service. Survey says...

Strongly agree	32%
Somewhat agree	41%
Somewhat disagree	15%
Strongly disagree	11%

Then, some spoilsport at Yankelovich Partners, Inc., the folks who actually did the survey, decided to throw in this statement..."I feel that the prices I pay now for goods and services entitle me to the highest level of customer service." Survey says...

Strongly agree	55%
Somewhat agree	34%
Somewhat disagree	6%
Strongly disagree	3%

Okay. The customer says that he or she is willing to pay more for better service. That's the good news. The bad news is that your customer thinks that you are already charging enough to provide a high level of customer service. Plus, the customer thinks that service isn't all that hot in many cases, partially because it really isn't and partially because they have come to expect more and are disappointed when they don't get it.

So there! What are you going to do?

My solution is that if you intend to survive, and are already giving consistently good service, read this book carefully. If you are not already giving consistently good service, read this book twice...and then do something!

2

THE REST OF THE STORY

Whenever you hear the word customer, don't make the mistake of thinking only about the folks on the opposite side of the counter or on the other end of the phone line. Think also about those internal customers who, through their emotional and physical efforts, make having folks on the other side of the counter possible. This book isn't as much about serving external customers as it is about serving and leading those "internal" customers who make the world work.

Here's a survey question that we did not ask but should have…"How much influence do you think you have over the way you are managed?" And here's another…"How much does the way you are managed influence the quantity of work you do?" And how about this one…"How much does the way you are managed influence the quality of work that you do?" Or even, "If you were managed differently or not at all, by how much would your work improve or get worse?"

Even though we don't have the exact answers to these questions, there is data that leads us to at least a pretty good idea. In 1992, *American Demographics* magazine published an article that updated an older survey asking employees what they wanted from their jobs.

Before we give you the answers, why not take a swing at the survey yourself? Rank the following job attributes from one to fifteen in order of desirability with number one being the most desirable.

What Workers Want

____ Good health insurance and other benefits
____ Interesting work

_____ Job security
_____ Opportunity to learn new job skills
_____ Annual vacations of week or more
_____ Freedom to work independently
_____ Recognition from co-workers
_____ Having a job in which you can help others
_____ Limited job stress
_____ Regular hours, no nights or weekends
_____ High income
_____ Working close to home
_____ Work that is important to society
_____ Chances for promotion
_____ Contact with a lot of people

Take a second look at the list. It is already in the order of desirability!

Are you surprised that high wages wasn't the number one attraction?

Here's an even more enlightening thing to think about. Go back to the list and place a check mark next to items that you or your employer could provide at little or no cost at all. Amazing, isn't it?

We like to do our own asking without forcing a choice of job attributes. Usually we give the blank survey form that follows without any prompting or suggestions as to what could be considered a positive job attribute. Of course, we have, from experience, compiled a list of the most often listed job attributes. Take a look at our list of positive job attributes and, just for grins, try it on yourself. If you are brave, give one of the survey forms to your employees and see what happens!

Notice that we've added a little twist. We ask respondents to tell us not just what they would like from their job, but how important each attribute really is and how well each attribute is being satisfied. The results are often quite surprising!

(Attributes are listed in the order of most to least.)

Most Unprompted Mentions	Relative Importance	Relative Satisfaction
1. Pay and benefits	Fun work environment	Leadership
2. Personal time	Personal growth	Personal time
3. Fun work environment	Opportunity to advance	Feedback
4. Empowerment	Reward/recognition	Reward/recognition
5. Reward/recognition	Empowerment	Pay/benefits
6. Personal growth	Training	Personal growth
7. Training	Leadership	Empowerment
8. Opportunity to advance	Pay/benefits	Fun environment

9. Feedback	Feedback	Advancement
10. Leadership	Personal time	Training

Job Attribute Survey

List the attributes that you would most like in a job. Rank them in the order of preference with number one being the most desirable, number two the next and so on. In the right column, score each attribute according to how well you have been satisfied in each category. If you are very satisfied, score the attribute as 10. If you are not satisfied at all, score it as a 0. (Unlike the attribute rank, more than one attribute can have the same score.)

Rank	Job Attribute	Score
_____	_____	_____
_____	_____	_____
_____	_____	_____
_____	_____	_____
_____	_____	_____
_____	_____	_____
_____	_____	_____
_____	_____	_____
_____	_____	_____
_____	_____	_____

IDEA STARTERS

Are you having a tough time thinking of job attributes that would really turn you on? Try this list for a few ideas.

Great pay and benefits	Opportunity to advance
Opportunity for personal growth	Recognition by peers
Recognition by industry leaders	Fun work environment
Job security	Personal time
Challenging work	Training and development
Great leadership	Feedback on personal performance
Empowered work environment	Customer interaction
Pleasant work environment	Fair treatment
Freedom from politics	Flexible hours
Work at or near home	Opportunity to be creative
Work with friends	Variety
Work with a respected company	Opportunity to travel
Participate w/trade associations	Having my opinion count
Family-centered work environment	Work w/state-of-the-art equipment

You can continue to add to the list although, after a while, new attributes become more and more difficult to distinguish from those already on the list. Here's a tip...once your employees have completed this exercise, you will have in black-and-white exactly what it will take to turn them on. (This could be the most valuable internal consumer data you could possibly acquire.)

ON YOUR OWN

There is only so much you can expect to learn from simple surveying. No matter how well you construct the instrument or how often you survey, there are some things that are as difficult to ask as they are difficult to tell. Occasionally you must resort to face-to-face communication.

Some questions require the practiced eye of the professional insider. Here is an important list that we will consider again later in great detail...

> How is performance rewarded?
>
> How is the company culture communicated?
>
> Who are the leaders both informal and formal?
>
> How is service modeled and who are the best models?
>
> What are the traditions?
>
> What are the sacred cows and to whom do they belong?
>
> Why are things done the way they are done?
>
> Who are the company thinkers?
>
> Who are the doers, the naysayers, the politicians?
>
> Again, who are the politicians?
>
> How are communications handled?
>
> What is the media? Who initiates and who controls what goes up and what filters down?

If you are serious about developing customer eyes, you must be willing to become a professional questioner. Consultants are really nothing more than professional questioners. It is true; they do use your watch to tell you what time it is. But we sometimes need consultants to ask the tough questions and bear the harsh answers. If the reaction is more than we can handle, we just fire 'em.

3

PUBLIC...AND PRIVATE RELATIONS

In the best of all worlds, public relations are personal relations. What was it that we're missing when we long for the customer service of the good old days? I know! We miss being called by name. We miss knowing the lady behind the counter as Mrs. Malobabich, or Smith or Washington. When we talked about the neighborhood store, we were talking about real neighbors. Sometimes the proprietors lived upstairs. We went to school with their kids and stopped in on Halloween for a treat of penny candy.

These are the good old days. That's what the Carole King song reminds us. There is no point in bemoaning days gone by. If our days are to be counted among the good, old days, it's up to us.

In the old days, nearly every business was a Ma and Pa business. Guess what? Every business is a Ma and Pa business! No matter who is in charge you can pretty much bet that it's somebody's Ma or Pa.

The challenge for big business is to love on customers as though they were the next-door neighbor of somebody's corner store. For small business the challenge is to do what the big guys can only do with great difficulty. If there is bad news for the little guy, it is that the big boys are getting better and better at listening to and responding to their customers, your customers.

HIGH-TECH FRIENDS

One thing that computers are great at is remembering. Put the data in and it's yours to use or lose. Too many companies collect data by the bucket and never take it out to work. Well, time to make the donuts! Put the data to work building close customer relationships.

Do this. Start right now collecting actionable data from your customers. The obvious is simple demographic data. Things like name, address and so on. Begin to gather the more useful information such as hobbies, type of work, purchase-history, even comments that may be of use, whatever your imagination says may lead you to a closer relationship with your customers.

One of our customers mentioned a potential transfer of her spouse. Jim looked into our database to see if there might be a compatible job match, faxed a short list of potentials in the new city and within a matter of weeks, our former client contact became our new client contact. And the number one promoter of T. Scott Gross and Company! The cost? Next to nothing.

High-tech allows even the majors to establish one-to-one relationships with their customers. When they get good at it, watch out.

Using transaction data, it is now possible to discover exactly who your customer is. When you know what one of them looks like, you can catch more that look just like her.

Marketing is the phrase coined by Don Peppers and Martha Rogers to describe the new age of relationship marketing. They suggest that technology (really we could have done this all along) allows us to develop long-term relationships with our customers. The goal, they say, is to gather longitudinal data, data over the long run about individual customers rather than the common practice of gathering snapshot information about a mass market.

We establish this long-term relationship with the idea in mind of capturing a larger share of customers. This is a dramatic departure from traditional efforts to capture share of market. What's the advantage? Simple. It is considerably more efficient to sell new products to old customers than to find new customers for old products.

With quality longitudinal data, we can begin to differentiate between the more valuable "regulars" and the less profitable single-transaction customers. We can also place a value on any individual customer based on sales volume, frequency and margin on the purchase. With this data we can create customized, even individualized marketing strategies and campaigns.

We can know what is appropriate to spend on customer maintenance and on whom to spend. We can even predict which of our current customers have a higher potential value. If we decide to try traditional mass media, we'll be able to target our efforts and achieve greater returns.

All this for the asking. And, you do have to ask.

New marketing is about dialogue with the customer. We do more than talk via the electronic media. We listen by telephone, by survey, in person, just like Ma and Pa at the neighborhood store, only now we're even better at handling what we learn.

The new market rules go far beyond recruiting new customers. With a value placed on customers as individuals, smart marketers (and we're all in marketing), will begin to think in terms of customer retention and customer recovery.

Every customer in every company should be in the database and be assigned a personal service manager.

The organization should actively court the big spenders for recruitment, retention and recovery and let the marginal and losing transactions go.

Also out the window is the idea of discounting.

Remember, anyone can give product away: it takes brains to sell it.

Marketing is nothing more than matchmaking gone commercial. Find out what customers need your product and simply make it available on terms that please. The new-think reminds us that once we have a customer, we can continue the relationship by reversing the process. Find out what your customers want and then find and offer the product and service they have in-so-many-words told us that they are ready to buy. Simple. Not easy.

This should help us avoid the dreaded "D" word, discount.

An interesting graph in *Fortune* magazine really put discounting into perspective for me. It showed that if you and your competitor both produce a similar product and both have total selling costs of 90 percent of the sales price (I know that this model won't fit every industry, but follow along and you'll still get the point), gross profit for both is 10 percent.

Let's say that one of you gets the bright idea to discount a modest 3.5 percent, hardly enough in some case to be noticeable by the customer. But look what that modest 3.5 percent does to your bottom line.. Profits fall an awesome 35 percent.

Do you want to do that every day?

And, in most cases, for the discount to be a real head-turner, you'll have to go to a lot deeper than 3.5 percent. Think about it.

Peppers and Rogers say it the best. "Discounting creates short-term market share, purchased from our competitors or borrowed against our own future sales and profits."

Successful entrepreneurs spend nearly 40 percent of their time marketing.

Years ago, if you had told me that I would end up being a sales-and-marketing person, I would have been more than surprised; I would have been offended.

President Clinton reportedly has a sign on his desk that says, "It's the economy, Stupid!" If I were to put a sign on my desk, or yours, it would say, "It's the marketing!"

Well, as long as we are going to spend so much effort marketing, we may as well involve the customer and have as our goal the establishment of long-term relationships. Carl Sewell wrote about creating customers for life. I think we need to be careful in our marketing to find, in the first place, customers who qualify for that kind of relationship.

LET'S GET PERSONAL

With the help of computer technology, every customer could and should be the individual responsibility of a team player. There should never be an unassigned customer floating in the database. Obviously, in some types of businesses, the ratio of customers to team players may be near unmanageable. At the very least, each customer should know the name of someone who is directly responsible for their continued satisfaction.

More important than speed, more important than convenience and often more important than how well the product performs is that all-important attribute, personal service. Everyone wants to be treated as an individual. Everyone is looking for status.

Being remembered by name by the owner makes higher prices "worth it." Being recognized by the employees tells you that you are special because you are so memorable.

At Lex Brodie's Tires in Honolulu, customers are usually greeted by name, yet they have thousands of customers, many of whom are seen only every three or four years.

How do they do it? Simple. Technology. When customers pull into the parking lot, sharp-eyed service managers enter their license-plate numbers into the curbside computer. Up pops the customer name, a short description for accuracy and a list of previous service and purchases.

Now it's easy to look like a mentalist. Lex Brodie's is packed with customers. They don't have the prettiest place in town. They don't have the lowest prices. But they do know their customers. And that makes the difference.

The best performing operations...encourage personal contact.

Tony Clemente, of Thrifty Car Rental and a reader of *Positively Outrageous Service,* sat beside me on a flight into Canada. He was beside himself as he shared a story about buying a shirt in Arlington, Texas. You wouldn't think that buying a shirt would be the highlight of a three-day trip, but it was.

It seems that when Tony went looking for a shirt, the concierge of his hotel recommended a local independent men's store. The prices were far from inexpensive and although their quality was top-notch, it was the personal service that made the visit memorable. In fact, Tony was treated so well that he spent nearly three hours and an untold amount of money. Why? (We all want to be loved and that's not so wrong.)

Dollars to donuts, when Tony walks back into that store, he will be remembered.

Maybe it's Dallas. Are we friendlier in Texas? We've had the same experience buying boots at Cowtown Boots in north Dallas. It was hot, so were we. I wanted boots but not shopping.

"Go ahead," encouraged Melanie. "At least look."

I have feet that are approximately a mile long and three-inches wide. Tough to fit to say the least. Dan Post makes distressed leather boots that had left me drooling for months. Too bad. Long, skinny, flatter-than-a-pancake feet just settle for what they've got.

We weren't five feet in the door when a friendly fellow stuck out his paw and said, "Gee you look thirsty! Would you like a cold beer, soda or even a glass of iced tea?" The truth is I had been "rode hard and put up wet." And a cold drink did seem like the perfect remedy. And they did have a lot of great-looking boots even if I knew none would fit me.

But at least trying them on in a nice cool environment would take the edge off a long day.

I walked out wearing the most beautiful pair of boots Dan Post ever made! And Tony Rodriguez said, "If they don't fit like a glove after you've walked in them for a while, send them back and I'll ship another size right away."

You can bet I'll be a regular at Cowtown Boots even if it's just to stop for a cold one.

You can't begin to do relationship marketing until you have the data. A current ad for IBM mentions Mitchells of Westport where they use an IBM data system to create relationship-marketing events for their customers. When new styles in tennis clothes arrive at the shop, customers who are known to be tennis players, get a special notice. And the rest of the database is left to wait its turn for items of interest, special interest, to them.

And special may very well be the key word. Customers feel special when they are singled out, when they are remembered.

Let's Get Involved

Positively Outrageous Servvice is about involving customers in their own service and marketing. One now-common approach is the use of toll-free numbers. In fact, two-thirds of American manufacturers use toll-free numbers for a portion of their product lines.

If there is one good reason for using an 800-number, it has to be the benefit of getting immediate feedback, feedback that is not only useful for marketing and product-development purposes, but also useful in situations where there may be a potential for product liability. Find out fast and you can move fast.

Of course, you also get complaints. In fact, when companies add a toll-free line for customers, complaints usually triple. But think about it. Which would you rather have? Lots of complaints and the opportunity to respond to them, or customers who decide that complaining to you is not worth the hassle and find it easier to take their complaints and their business somewhere else?

Those with complaints that are successfully resolved are likely to tell five others and be even more loyal than those with unresolved complaints. And unresolved complaints can create at least nine unfavorable mentions to friends and strangers.

4

CUSTOMER FEEDBACK SYSTEMS

Customer feedback systems can be sophisticated or as simple as what some operators refer to as "working in the floor."

What many managers miss is too often their feedback systems don't work hard enough. They either don't produce the right data or they fail to produce quality information. The biggest failure is in pinpointing customer expectations.

We may ask, "Was everything alright?" and get a "Yes" for an answer. But what if the customer expected something more than "alright?" What if the customer expected "spectacular?" If that is the case, then "alright" represents horrible failure.

Every survey, whether written or verbal needs a scale to help define expectations.

What Our Customers Experience	Importance	Performance
High level of reliability	1 2 3 4 5	1 2 3 4 5

Asking questions without follow up to probe for more and get a handle on the relative importance of the attribute is the same as interviewing yourself.

And while we're at it, there is not one survey that is the mother of all surveys. Create special surveys for special occasions. We'll show you a couple of written versions and you can choose the format that works best for the situation.

DON'T YOU HATE IT WHEN THAT HAPPENS?

How about fishing for complaints? Sometimes a survey should get right to the point and ask, "What's buggin ya?"

Occasionally we go on a seek-and-destroy mission to ferret out micro-insults, those little things that make you crazy. Micro-insults are policies that tell internal customers that they are not trusted. They make traditional customers do things that are inconvenient or demeaning. Things like...

> ➤ Two entry doors but one is always locked. (It's the one you try to use first!)
> ➤ Voice mail that asks you to spell the name of your party using the keypad.
> ➤ Empty employee-of-the-month parking spaces, right by the door — and it's storming!
> ➤ Salesclerks who answer the telephone while waiting on you and they serve that customer!
> ➤ Salesclerks who continue personal phone calls while you wait to ask for help.
> ➤ Over-stuffed paper towel dispensers that produce confetti instead of dry hands.
> ➤ "No substitutions."
> ➤ Toilets that flush automatically and have their own ideas about when.
> ➤ A bank of pay phones all mounted at a back-breaking three feet.
> ➤ Companies that refuse to give you a price saying that "someone will call you back."
> ➤ Spending or authorization limits that are so low they are demeaning.
> ➤ Reserved parking spaces. Period.
> ➤ Order here, pick up in the next county signs.
> ➤ Serpentine lines two miles long when there are no customers.

Can you add a few? Of course!

Too often when we create customer feedback systems, we focus on the big stuff and forget that everyone is doing a good job on the big stuff. It's the little things that make the difference.

Call WordPerfect for software support. I hate calling for software support but if I have to call anywhere, the folks at WP are the best. Someone who also hates to wait in telephone queues created a WordPerfect hold-jockey. While you wait, the hold-jockey plays pleasant music and periodically tells you how long is the average wait and how many customers are ahead of you.

They took most of the pain out of waiting.

Our friends at Boccone's have been very concerned about the length of time their customers sometimes have to wait. (Well, it is worth it!)

Why not make waiting part of the experience? You could bring out a few somethings to snack on, let the entertainers wander outside from time to time and even put up a big board to keep waiting customers posted on how long they can expect to wait. That should eliminate the folks who keep coming up to see if it's almost their turn. You could even call out their name occasionally..."Smith. Party of two. Not yet!"

RECAPTURING DEFECTORS

What about customers who have become inactive? The forgotten ones are those who just don't come back. For whatever reason, some customers just stop coming in. They're not angry. They haven't been mistreated. They've just found someone who makes them happier.

You're choice is to let them go and look for replacements or get them back. What's it going to be? Getting them back may be the least expensive alternative but it's not even a consideration if you don't realize that they are gone.

What is your customer retention rate? Or in the reverse, what is your customer defection rate?

OH, REALLY?

It is rare for customers and management to share the same perception of customer service. One client reported that they were first and foremost a "people" company. The world, according to their employees, was quite another planet. When we talked with employees, they told us over and over that management was repressive, controlling and that they would gladly trade a portion of their generous compensation package for the ability to work independently, to be able to talk with the boss and have him actually listen.

The boss's office was lined with the latest pop-management books, many signed by the authors. The walls were lined with certificates of completion from many of the most respected training seminars. But talking the talk is one thing; walking the talk quite another.

If you are serious about service, start with the service that you provide the servers.

Hay Research for Management discovered that of 750,000 managers, only 55 percent are willing to characterize their company as a good place to work. Only 35 percent believe that top management actually listens to their complaints. Figures. Only 59 percent of top corporations actually survey their customers. (I guess it figures that if you don't ask, you probably aren't interested in the answer.)

It's a funny thing. Unhappy team members just don't do much to delight the customer. The flip side of that is that happy customers also lead to happy team players.

Why? It's easier to work where the customers are happy.

ARE WE EASY TO DO BUSINESS WITH?

If there is one thing business ought to want to know, it is whether or not they have made it easy to do business. We erect some of the most unexpected obstacles and then wonder why customers find somewhere else to take their business.

Read on!

Service Selection Guide

➤ Are you open when the customer wants to shop or needs service?
➤ Do you offer one-stop solutions to customer problems?
➤ Will you special order or otherwise accommodate unusual requests?
➤ Is the delivery system for product and service convenient and speedy?
➤ Do you provide installation and post-purchase support?
➤ Is the entire staff trained to solve problems or are there only a few "specialists?"
➤ Are the prices fair and competitive?
➤ Do you make it easy to pay?
➤ Do you have a "no questions asked" return policy?
➤ How easy is it to place an order?
➤ Do I have a choice in how I buy? Walk in, telephone, fax, mail, modem, drive-thru.
➤ How often and for how long can I expect to wait?
➤ Do you offer only top quality products?

➤ Do you offer a variety of solutions to my problems?

➤ Do you treat me as a number or as a valuable long-term friend of the firm?

➤ Do you present a clean, professional physical environment?

➤ Do I want to be known by your reputation?

A customer of ours, Steven Varga of Diversified Employment Services, copied us on a letter that he wrote to what now must be a former supplier...

"I have been a customer of yours for about a year...called to order one box of plain certificates...was shocked to learn...that your company no longer accepts orders of less than thirty dollars...as a supposed 'valued customer' and one who has read your catalog cover which speaks about 'customer service', I can only say you redefine the phrase..."

Dr. William D. Wilsted of Ernst and Young says that the buyer's and seller's perceptions of quality are often mirror images. He measures quality in three dimensions...

Effective...does the product perform as advertised?

Responsive...did the company deliver on time?

Personal...was the service as expected?

Seller's viewpoint		Customer's point of view
10%	PERSONAL	70%
20%	RESPONSIVE	20%
70%	EFFECTIVE	10%

CUSTOMER EYES

Be your own mystery shopper. Sounds like an ad where you might find a magnifying glass and a decoder ring. However it may sound, it's good advice for managers to begin to look at customer service through "customer eyes." Unfortunately, sometimes even the customers don't know how to put into words how they feel about your company and why they feel that way. In those cases or when you want to be totally objective, an outside professional shopper firm may be the best bet.

When shopping for outside help, there are a few tips to keep in mind...

Mystery Shoppers are reporters, not consultants. Asking professional shoppers to provide consulting may or may not be within their capability. If you want consulting as part of the service, make certain that you are working with a company that specializes in your industry.

Shopping may come naturally to the typical American but you're not looking for a typical shopper. You need trained specialists who will bring back objective data.

Basing compensation on a few mystery shopping reports can be worse than unfair; it can be totally demoralizing.

CUSTOMER MAINTENANCE

Do you need a reason for creating a customer maintenance program? Here are six!

> ➤ Marketing is expensive. It's cheaper to keep old customers than to find new.
> ➤ Long-term customers spend more. A credit card holder is worth about $100 after one year but $300 after five.
> ➤ Long-term customers are walking testimonials. They bring new business.
> ➤ Satisfied customers mean happy employees. Productivity improves.
> ➤ Satisfied customers lead to lower turnover and training costs.
> ➤ Long-term customers already understand your business, this saves time.

We've already talked about assigning customers to team players and about using the database to sound the alarm when a customer stops buying. What else can you do to retain customers? The best advice my loyal readers have heard. It's called Positively Outrageous Service or POS.

POS is service that...

> ➤ is random and unexpected;
> ➤ is out-of-proportion to the circumstance;
> ➤ invites the customer to play or be otherwise involved; and
> ➤ creates positive, compelling word-of-mouth.

A few other favorite descriptions...POS is the service story that you can't wait to tell. It is making your customer say WOW!

It's also the act of shmushing your marketing right up to your cash register. In fact, when you begin to have difficulty telling where your marketing stops and your service begins...that's Positively Outrageous Service.

Read about POS in another chapter. Right now we need to think about when to give POS. What opportunities could you take advantage of to surprise and delight your customers?

CUSTOMER FEEDBACK SYSTEMS

OPPORTUNITIES FOR POS

➤ When customers are waiting. (What could you do to make waiting part of the experience? What could you do to make waiting fun?)

➤ When customers have a complaint. (What could you do to turn a complaint into an event?)

➤ Just for the heck of it. (What small surprise could you orchestrate to let your customers know that they are important?)

➤ After the sale. (What could you do, in that time when customers often feel as though they have been forgotten?)

Here is an idea or two, just to get you started.

Waiting...our friends who run the Subway Sandwich Shop in Selma, Alabama, have discovered a unique way to make waiting pay. Some days when the line is long, they pass out tickets and hold a drawing good for a free Subway sandwich on the next visit. Can't you just see the regular customers when the line starts to grow and they suspect a freebie day? I bet they tell newcomers, "Go ahead. I'm not in a hurry!"

Complaints...everyone is so afraid that if they get a reputation for doing whatever it takes to make things right when things go wrong, that some customers may take advantage of them. Of course, they will! But should you worry about it? Not even. (That's why there's hell!)

One night a lady called our restaurant and my brother Stuart answered the phone. She proceeded to eat him alive saying that her chicken had not been delivered and that she had ordered over an hour and a half earlier . She was, according to her, a personal friend of Stan Gross.

"...And I know that it's Stan's policy that when things are messed up, the order goes out on the next truck and it goes out free. I'm expecting that to happen or I'll call Stan at home and he'll have your butt. Understand?"

"Yes, ma'am, " was Stuart's reply. "But I'm a little confused. There's a Scott Gross, a Steven Gross, a Stuart Gross and a Paul Stacy Gross. But, ma'am, there's no Stan Gross."

Long pause.

"Stuart. That's the one! I'm a personal friend of Stuart's."

"Speaking," Stu replied cheerfully.

She hung up.

Just Because...Sometimes, and always on a completely random basis, when we encounter an especially nice customer, Mom will toss in an extra book, comp a video tape or maybe even throw in a candy bar. They never know if or when. But you can bet that when it happens, they tell the world. The Cajuns call it lagniappe. We call it POS.

After the sale...Have you ever felt like you've been thrown out the door after the purchase? Discarded as trash because you ran out of money? Sometimes, after the sale is the best time to take a client to dinner or remember them with some small gift or service.

Southwest Airlines puts postcards and mailing addresses of customers where employees on break can jot a quick thank-you note to customers from just completed flights. Nice touch. But then, SWA is the only profitable major airline. Can you think of the reason? They give POS!

"Random" My Favorite Word

What makes relationship marketing so special is that the customer never knows exactly what to expect other than to be remembered. "Random and unexpected" describes the psychological underpinnings of Positively Outrageous Service. When customers never quite know what to expect other than that the service and product will be good, they keep coming back.

Retaining Those All Important Internal Customers

Do this:

> ➤ Walk the floor to survey informally...know everyone by name.
> ➤ Occasionally survey formally...get professional assistance if necessary.
> ➤ Create events, reasons to celebrate and things to look forward to.
> ➤ Become a master of surprises.
> ➤ Make certain that your players have plenty of opportunity to speak out.
> ➤ Respond to every suggestion...no form letters.
> ➤ Eliminate stress by providing training, tools and time to do the job right.

What Does it Cost?

If you haven't calculated the value of a lifetime customer, do it right now. Figure the average purchase. Add a factor for potentially increased sales.

Estimate the value to future sale of the business and don't forget the potential for positive word-of-mouth. Consider some impact on employee retention and add a fudge factor for knowing your system, even suggesting new products. Balance all this against marketing, training and the cost of errors and returns and see if you don't get a fairly large number.

We did this while working with our friends at Thrifty Car Rental. I won't tell you the number but it was a big one. Don Himelfarb, their leader, had been pushing for greater authority for Customer Service Representatives in the handling of customer complaints. After seeing the value of a happy customer, Don got little argument.

And neither will you once you put a pen to paper and discover just how much poor service can cost.

Don discovered that 85 percent of the customers who called corporate with a complaint didn't even suggest monetary compensation!

Get it? Fixing complaints isn't expensive and not fixing them can cost you the entire enchilada. All told, Thrifty figured that pleasing the customer had a cost of a paltry $.035 per transaction. That's nothing more than the biggest value in business. Satisfied customers for less than a nickel a piece. If you could buy them on the open market, you'd order a million. Well, they're standing at your counter, yours for the asking.

IN CLOSING...

When our minister says that, he doesn't mean that he's about to finish — only that the thought has crossed his mind...too. When I say it, we're real close.

Ask this...

> ➤ Do you "shop" your competition? This is benchmarking in its basic form.
> ➤ Do you actively seek ideas from other industries? This is parallel analysis.
> ➤ Do you have both passive and active customer feedback systems?
> ➤ Do you actively research your customer base and your market?
> ➤ Do you have a customer retention program such as frequent buyer, etc?
> ➤ Do you know when you lose a customer and actively pursue them?
> ➤ Do you survey non-users?

➤ Do you have an aggressive product and service development effort?

➤ Do you get useful data from MIS and do you use it to its fullest?

➤ Do you have a "whatever it takes" complaint resolution system?

DO THIS...

➤ Target your potential customers carefully. High-margin companies usually play to a fairly homogenous customer base. You really can't be all things to all people.

➤ Once you win your customers, do whatever it takes to get to know them.

➤ Stand out with great service. Be known for solving problems.

➤ Don't let a good customer get away. Not a traditional customer. Not an internal customer.

➤ Love on employees who love on customers. Do business with nice people.

PART IV

MEASURE

1

SIX OF ONE...

MEASURING SERVICE QUALITY...
THE WORST CHAPTER IN THIS BOOK!

A rat you can feed cheese. You can even catch rats with cheese. Much of our knowledge of human behavior was developed based on experiments with rats. Many of those experiments involved simple behavior-response systems where a desired behavior was rewarded with cheese or some other rat delicacy. Employees are not rats.

Measuring service with the ultimate idea in mind that we will use the information to shape employee behavior is fundamentally wrong. Sometimes people, and maybe even rats, do things just for the heck of it.

You can argue, if you like, that even if we can't immediately see how employees find reward in the work itself there still must be a reward. Somewhere. Somehow. Something. And, some will say, that reward is not much different than a chunk of cheddar. Okay, have it your way. For me there are some things worth doing just because they are the right thing to do. Some things are worth doing because they, for whatever reason, fill the soul. And I don't suspect lab rats of having soul. They hardly manage to reach "cute and cuddly." "Soulful" just doesn't seem to fit.

People, even though they do some of the dumbest things from time to time, still stand head and whiskers over lab rats. I think it's entirely appropriate to begin this discussion with a reminder that all the measuring and prodding in the world won't be enough to make people fall in love with work that has been stripped of its purpose.

There are two jobs I absolutely hate, stacking cheese and painting. In restaurants, we used to stack the cheese slices to make them easier to separate when cooking burgers. (There's a real one-of-a-kind "no brainer" that makes me cringe at the very thought.)

Painting is right on up there in the same nasty category. B-O-R-I-N-G. And, seemingly without purpose to boot.

Yet, there have been a few times when I have caught myself smiling, sometimes even singing while doing both. Cooking burgers for company makes me happy and the idea of stacking cheese for our visiting army seems almost a privilege. And painting? Well, I can't think of an example but there must be one!

Get it? Rats can't plan for tomorrow. Rats can't think far enough beyond the moment to sacrifice immediate pleasure for a long-term greater pleasure or reward. But people can and do. Everyday we see people sacrificing for ideas and others. We see Moms and Dads going without so that they may experience the greater joy of watching their youngsters do well.

Read on, if you will. Learn what you can about measuring service performance in terms of customer satisfaction. Keep in mind that the better goal of measurement in the work environment is not to discover some neat-o rat and cheese arrangement that will make work go better or faster. Be on the lookout instead for ways to make the work itself have value. Look for opportunities to make work a source of pure joy.

When employees hear that the company, make that the boss, is about to measure customer satisfaction, they quickly translate customer satisfaction to mean "employee performance." And they just as quickly decide that they could live just fine without it, thank-you very much. It is true that there is a pretty solid linkage between customer satisfaction and employee performance. The point that most employees and many managers miss is that a measure of customer satisfaction also provides a pretty good picture of the system under which the service is delivered.

Whether you want to say that you are measuring employee performance or the efficiency of the system in which service is provided, it's really a matter of six of one, half a dozen of the other...as long as you know the difference!

What scares the bejeebers out of employees is that while they intuitively realize that performance is highly dependent on the service or manufacturing process, they aren't quite so certain that you have reached that same conclusion. They don't want you to be confused into thinking that poor performance is necessarily due solely to slothful work habits. While measuring the output of a packaging machine or evaluating an automatic press for speed, accuracy and quality is fairly straightforward, deciding when an employee has given "friendly, courteous service" is a horse of another color.

For you, the manager, the toughest part of all seems to be knowing where to start.

Managers know they should be measuring some things more than things you can read from a good profit and loss statement. They just don't know what.

We'll focus on those attributes that you are not likely to learn in a book on accounting or hear in a lecture on industrial engineering. Our numbers will be just as important to the conduct of business and will ultimately have a critical impact on the bottom line. And they will be crucial to another form of engineering, job process engineering. But they will reflect the softer focus of service as perceived by the customer.

To avoid muddying the waters, we'll skip for now discussion of measuring service as perceived by the internal customer. Know that the rules apply equally on either side of the cash register or desk.

MEASURE, MEASURE EVERYWHERE, AND NOT A THOUGHT TO THINK

The toughest thing is to measure customer service.

The first step is to make service as tangible as possible. We are accustomed to thinking strictly in terms of hard goods. Fine. But this economy is a service economy. And the idea that intangibles can't be measured has to go.

This is even easier done than said once you get into the habit of thinking in terms of measuring. Start listing ways to measure service and there is no stopping. Even marketing types have begun to evaluate sponsorships in terms of cost for comparable coverage as they measure mentions and lines of copy compared with the cost of purchasing the same amount.

Of course, there are some things that are easier than others to measure and there are some things not worth the time to measure. Overall, measuring service is just not that big of a deal. It is deciding how you will put that measurement to work that takes the noodling.

Let's start right off with the toughest part of measuring service...deciding what to measure. If there is anything that throws managers into a panic, it is the problem of measuring seeming intangibles. We all know how to measure profit, or the lack of it. We know how to calculate inventory turn and cost of capital. And we've all been nailed to the wall over travel expenses that exceeded the per diem established by policy. But service? Performance? You've got to be kidding!

No, we're not.

You can measure customer service, job satisfaction, the value of attending a seminar, anything you want. Let's go for a few examples just to get the juices flowing. Pick an industry, any industry. You want lodging? Dry cleaners? Airlines? Doctors? Manufacturing?

Okay, you've got it. Just remember that some measures of product quality also reflect the quality of service. More accurately, instead of pretending that we are purely measuring service, let's talk in terms of customer satisfaction. That's because customer satisfaction extends beyond the bounds of fast, polite, service personnel to include the less corporeal attributes of quality and value.

For the sake of argument, we'll attempt to stick to service. (We admit that the line is often blurry and ask forgiveness in advance for straying.)

Lodging

Financial performance could include:

Revenue per room

Revenue per employee

Occupancy rate

Average rate

Percentage of guests who pay the published or "rack" rate

Percentage who receive a discount

Old-fashioned return on investment

Service:

Percentage of repeat guests

Percentage of guests who use the restaurant or lounge

Number of complaints

Number of rings before a guest's call is answered

Percentage of guests who make additional reservations during check out

Percentage of your guest's lodging visits you get

How your guests rank your property compared to the competition

Percentage of guest comment cards that are positive compared to those that are negative

Percentage of time when requested room is available

Percentage of stays that are extended

Percentage of customers upgraded because the requested room was not available...or total costs incurred due to lack of requested product (cost of conversion)

Room rate adjustments

Restaurant capture

Restaurants

Service:

Percentage of guests addressed by name

Percentage of "on deal" sales

Time from seating to order to delivery

Customers per hour

Product temperature

Product taste as judged by diner

Number of orders requiring rework

Number of trips to the table required to complete service

Gratuities

Frequency

Professional Presentor

Knowledge of subject

Ability to adapt to audience needs

Ability to customize presentation and resource materials

Ability to use humor

Involves the audience

Pre-presentation contact

Ideas presented are useful in present form

Ability to control environment and respond to distractions

Ability to encourage and respond to questions

Pace, style and presence

Skillful and appropriate use of audio/visual equipment and materials

Hairstylist

Frequency of visits

Annual turnover or customer retention percentage

Percentage of customers who tip

Percentage of customers who request a specific stylist

Percentage of new customers who are referrals

Average tip amount

Grocery

Percentage of direction requests answered by a personal escort to the merchandise

Percentage of customers greeted by name or thanked by name when paying by check or card

Length of time required to wait at check out

Physician

Percentage of new customers who are referrals

Satisfaction as measured by survey

Percentage of patients who schedule "checkup" visits

Percentage of patients who request second opinions for major procedures

Percentage of families served where both spouses are patients

Percentage of patients who return for additional treatment due to misdiagnosis or complications

Percentage of patients who die on the operating table

Ability to contact the doctor when the office is closed

Office staff's ability to keep appointments on schedule

Courtesy of the office staff

Subjective measure of "bedside manner"

Percentage who would recommend the practice to others (considered by a majority of Americans to be the most important indicator)

Manufacturer

Man hours per unit

Percentage of or value of scrap materials

Orders shipped on time

Percentage of time line is running

Average time required to change over to another product

Sales

Average number of new, qualified prospects per week

Average number of prospects who become clients per week

New accounts as a percentage of

total accounts

Average length of time to convert a prospect to a sale

Percentage of customers who are repeat customers

Average cost of sale

Personal

Hours per week spent with spouse/children

Hours per week spent exercising

Percentage of pay that is saved or invested

Hours spent per week in community service

Airline

Percentage of customer's total air travel booked with you when there is a choice

Satisfaction as reported by survey in comparison to other airlines

Ratio of happy letters to complaint letters

Number of complaints per thousand passengers

Number of complaints per thousand passenger miles

Record of on-time departures and arrivals

Number of lost bags per thousand

Percentage of passengers who pay full fare

Insurance Company...broadline

Number of referrals

Customer retention at renewal

Number of complaints to the insurance commission

Percentage of customers who purchase additional policies

Customer satisfaction as revealed by formal survey

Average time to settle claim

Percentage of disputed claim settlements

Wholesale Distributor

Customer retention

Percentage of delinquent accounts

Number of complaints per account

Accuracy of order fill

Accuracy of invoice

Number of property damage claims due to careless drivers

Heavy Equipment Manufacturer

Number of repeat customers

Average time to receive critical replacement parts

Average time required to complete field maintenance

Percentage of high-use parts in inventory

Percentage of reworks required for maintenance work

Number of defects per new unit

Average hours required for maintenance

Percentage of invoices that are accurate

Percentage of orders that are accurate

Dry Cleaner

Number of buttons broken/ replaced

Number of items returned for rework

Percentage of orders ready on time

Percentage of customers recognized by name

Percentage of garments lost

Supermarket

Percentage of items that scan properly

Average wait time at check out

Percentage of customers that are known by name

Percentage of merchandise bought on deal compared to percentage bought at full price

Frequency of visit

Percentage of customer's total grocery budget spent with you

Percentage of customers who are taken to products when they inquire about location

Satisfaction as reported by survey

Tele-service Operation

Percentage of customers not sold, "turndowns." (These, too, put a cost on the system.)

Average sale per transaction

Revenue per employee

Average time spent on hold

Percentage of orders completed accurately

Bureaucracy

Number of regulations written per hour

Average delay per project

Average number of forms per project

Average weight of forms per project

Average number of attorneys involved per project

Average number of disconnected calls per transfer attempt

Average number of times per day you can say, "That's not my department." ("That's not my job" earns credit only in unionized organizations.)

Number of supervisors per actual worker. (If this is a government department, this number should be as large as possible because, with government, the worst thing is that we would get what we pay for!)

And...the world famous, "Generic" category!

Number of transfers before reaching the person who can answer your question or solve your problem

Percentage of being called back when promised

Percentage of times actually getting to the boss/owner when requested

Length of time spent in resolving your problem

Percentage of times when called by name

Percentage of times reaching a human instead of voice mail

Percentage of times an 800-number was provided for resolving problems as well as taking your order

Number of pre-addressed, post-paid mailers sent

Number of drive-thru service operations provided

Revenue per unit

Percentage of times put on hold without permission

Percentage of correct and consistent answers received

And, as a "generic customer"

Reaching a human, not voice mail

Being put on hold without permission

Hours of operation convenient to your schedule

Convenient parking provided

Greeted immediately

Complete few forms, if any

Businesses accept various forms of payment

Ability to talk to a clerk without interruption

No hidden charges

Ability to get product assistance after the sale

Being given tips/training on product use or operation

Receiving full explanation of how problems happened while accepting responsibility

As you begin to think about what to measure in your organization, don't be fixated on creating a measurement system that covers everyone. It is rare that one measure will adequately fit an entire organization. Do be certain to measure service quality as perceived by both internal and traditional customers. Ignoring the internal customer is disaster because what makes internal customers dissatisfied eventually runs under the office door and oozes onto the showroom floor.

Taking care of internal customers is nothing more than being proactive in caring for your traditional customers.

In spite of the importance of measuring service quality, there are times when you should not. If you have no intention of putting the data to positive use, skip it. Measuring service quality does require effort that should not be wasted. Worse, when you measure, your team players will expect to see the results. They'll want to know how they stand.

Even customers who participate are entitled to see results. So measure only when there is a definite plan to take action.

Service quality feedback systems should have a limited life. That's not to say that you shouldn't always be involved with the process of measuring, only that the process itself should be allowed to evolve. As the system provides you with actionable data, and as changes are implemented in response, the measurement system should be allowed to change its focus.

Measuring service quality should be an ongoing process, a process that should consist of a series of measurement projects. Each measurement project should have a separate goal, a definite beginning and end. (There is no requirement to announce the end until the goal has been achieved.)

Even though we promised to hold off on a prolonged discussion of measuring internal service, why not back up and review that last category? How many of those measurements would be suitable for measuring your service to your internal customers? How would your employees rate your service to them based on some of those very same attributes?

2

INCH BY INCH...IT'S A CINCH!

Measuring performance isn't something that you do for blood sport. The purpose is not to see who you can catch in a mistake. Nope. Measuring has only three valid purposes:

1) To determine how to fairly reward great performance;
2) To discover where additional coaching may be needed; and
3) To learn where the system needs improvement.

People we reward and coach.
Systems get fixed.
Don't get that backwards!

WHAT IT IS...AND WHAT IT...

Customer satisfaction. Can you define it?

Some say that it is meeting or exceeding customer expectations. Good try!

Others say it can be expressed in terms of retention, frequency and customer share. Back to the bean counting for you!

Or you might think of it as a low ratio of complaints. Not even, Dude!

Customer satisfaction is whatever the individual customer says floats his or her boat. Get it? Customer Satisfaction is a highly individual even emotional matter. It is simply whatever pleases that customer at that moment. And worse, the very term "satisfaction" can be dangerous. Satisfied customers are customers whose basic needs are being met. They aren't necessarily WOWed. Their expectations may be being met but just barely.

If the goal is to maintain, customer satisfaction may be a perfectly reasonable goal. Otherwise, satisfied customers are what it takes to preserve your position but not increase market share. Customer satisfaction is to most folks an inferior standard. It is getting by to get by. Worse, "customer satisfaction" is a knife's-edge position because satisfied customers are just one step way from going elsewhere.

Who cares if customers are satisfied? We want to know exactly the depth of their feelings about our product and service. We want to make them say WOW! If all we know is that they are satisfied, we are certain to miss the opportunity to go the next step.

Simply satisfying customers cannot be called a competitive advantage. Any company that still has its doors open is satisfying at least some of its customers. (Some people will settle for anything.)

Satisfaction is easy. Quality is a notch up the ladder. Value is where it's at.

It is quite possible to score very high on quality and bomb completely in terms of value. The trick is to achieve the perfect balance between price and quality. It is service, Positively Outrageous Service, that tips the scale by adding perceived value on the customer's terms. That makes service a one-of-a-kind, customized, spur-of-the-moment product.

Service is an intangible product created for an individual customer at the point of sale.

Customer service leaders take great pains to ensure that team players understand that service is custom-created, one customer at a time and defined in customer terms. They also make a big deal out of explaining the relationship between great customer service and profitability.

We want to measure service quality, that perception of value that extends beyond mere minimum standards. Service quality, (we include the product as well), needs to be measured in terms of the competition and the other alternative, just not buying. In employee terms, this concept is well illustrated by the folks on public assistance who have discovered that the available jobs can't compete with the benefits provided by the government.

I was told of a conversation between two men, one who was an unemployed oil rig worker. He had been jobless for nearly three years. My friend pointed out that there were thousands of jobs that, although low paying, would nonetheless get him off the dole.

He reached for his wallet, extracted a plastic card and said, "I ain't workin' for no $5.00 an hour. They don't have no benefits. I can go to the hospital, take out this card, and the state pays my medical bills. All of 'em. I can't afford to work for no $5.00."

Good point.

Your customers and potential employees feel the same. Sometimes they just don't buy.

Measuring service quality is not a project. It is a process. Just as is the idea of pleasing customers not something that we do once in a while.

Although there is a strong correlation between perceived service quality and market share, there is no point in creating a service quality measurement system until the organization is 100 percent sold on the need to get started. Everyone must also be clear on the idea that everyone is a customer and everyone has customers. The measurement system has its underlying goal making the intangible idea of service tangible by presenting its picture in the form of reliable numbers. These numbers must have the confidence of management.

A well-constructed service quality measurement system is designed with the idea in mind that the data collected will enable management and team players alike to make informed decisions about quality. It will help get things done right the first time and reduce the more costly traditional approach of inspection and rework.

Quality and cost are not synonymous. They are not interchangeable nor are they always used mutually occurring. Simply spending more doesn't necessarily translate to a perception of higher quality. If you don't ask your customers what really matters...you won't know.

More important, service quality measurement will help eliminate the cost of doing the wrong things. We're not talking about eliminating screw-up. We're talking about not doing things that the customer doesn't care get done at all. These savings can fall straight to the bottom line.

Overspending on product and service that doesn't matter to the customer does absolutely nothing to enhance your position with the customer. And you'll never ever know about these potential savings unless you get in the habit of asking.

On a less positive note, when companies are forced to cut costs, if they have an effective service quality measurement system, they have at their disposal a system for deciding which cuts will yield the greatest savings with the least negative impact on the customer's perception of service quality.

Now, cuts can be made with a bit more finesse than whipping out the

Black and Deckers and hacking away at what to the customer is not fat at all but the very meat and bones that satisfy most.

By survey, only 5 percent of customers believe that business actually listens when they speak. This means that not only can you learn a lot by asking, you will gain the respect of your customers by the very fact that you ask. And if you show proof of actually listening, you'll flat blow them away!

WHY BOTHER?

The first step is not deciding what to measure. It is deciding why to measure.

There is no doubt that companies that consistently take the pulse of their customers are market leaders. But, when we ask new clients if they measure customer service and quality, the answer has been consistently an embarrassed, "No." Even companies that make a big, hairy deal, claiming that they are "customer driven", haven't done a thing to find out if they really are.

Yet it's so darned obvious that measuring service quality is more than important; it's a near-free resource that will tell management how to increase customer share, that is get more of not just the potential market, but more business from the customers you already have. And these customers don't have to be found, just wooed.

Even though People's Express, an employee-owned airline, bit the dust, they did a lot of things right. They put their executives in direct contact with the folks who paid the bills, the customers. Don Burr was quoted as saying, "Coffee stains on the flip down trays mean (to the customers) that we do our engine maintenance wrong."

Unfortunately, there is often a big difference between a company's service culture and the perception held by the customer. And where "that's-the-way-we've-always-done-it" is a part of the culture, all of the measurement in the world isn't going to count for much.

If there is one criticism that fits nearly every top executive of nearly every large firm, it is that they tend to assume that they have their finger on the pulse of the market. They think that having the big issues covered creates some sort of invincible competitive advantage while at the same time the details, those little things that mean so much to customers, are going straight to hell in a handcart. Because of this natural but totally off-base belief, service quality measurement must often be sold to the decision-makers. In fact, if you are a change agent in your organization, there is little use in dreaming up fabulous systems unless you are also a whiz at creating internal marketing.

In many companies you simply won't be taken seriously.

I remember going to a vice president of operations and telling him that our internal surveys indicated that we had on our hands a pretty disgruntled workforce. I suggested that we act on that data by creating a simple measurement system accompanied by an incentive program. We would target one or two very specific problems reported as significant by our customers.

"We already have an incentive program to take care of those issues," he said.

"We do?" I was pretty new and pretty intimidated. I thought I had missed something.

"Yep. They do their job and they get to keep it."

It was back to the marketing drawing board and back to praying for the god of enlightened management to visit the executive suite.

Al DeLiberto of Boccone's restaurant insists that the restrooms be cleaned every fifteen minutes because he knows if customers see dirt there, they "know" the kitchen is also a mess.

We are fond of saying that it is our job to be quality fanatics because everyone in the business does a credible job painting the big picture. The difference between the amateur and the pro lies in the details.

And just what could you learn?

You could learn...

➤ How your customer views your performance compared to the competition.
➤ How your industry performance compares with other industries.
➤ What the customer considers important as opposed to merely nice.
➤ How your customer views specific processes in the system.
➤ Of a competitive advantage that you did not realize that you had.
➤ Exactly how and why your customers make purchase decisions.
➤ New opportunities to create an industry product or service breakthrough.
➤ How to more effectively allocate resources.
➤ That you are wasting money to provide services that don't matter to the customer.
➤ How to stand out from the competition.

The ultimate goal of any service quality measurement system has to be found in the number of higher profit customers and highly effective team players retained, and the number of new ones attracted through positive word-of-mouth (reputation). The process is cheaper than marketing and cheaper than cheerfully accepting defective merchandise for return.

You could say that service quality measurement is never having to say you're sorry. Or almost never.

Actually, one common misconception is that service quality measurement, call it customer satisfaction measurement, if it makes you happy, has as its primary goal the retention of potentially unhappy customers. (These could be internal customers, don't forget.) But that's a problem of context.

Yes, listening to customers and jumping on their complaints like white on rice does indeed go a long way towards salvaging digruntled customers. The truly enlightened treat service quality measurement as a proactive tool. Service quality measurement is an awesome tactic for attracting customers and retaining them through enhanced relationships.

Service quality measurement is not an operation's panacea. Measuring alone does little to influence performance. What does make a difference is the correlation between perceived value and profitability. Despite whatever anecdotal evidence may exist (not denying that some consumers are indeed bottom feeders), companies that offer a quality product and quality service are able to charge more. And that means profitability.

Point: Unless you know what customers think is quality...as well as having an awareness of the attributes they view as unnecessary, you cannot efficiently provide that price-quality combination that translates into higher-margin sales.

"But our salespeople know our customers. They keep us informed and we respond."

The truth is closer to, "our customers aren't all that comfortable telling our salespeople how to improve our product." In fact, they don't think it's their responsibility to do our product development. They just go away, riding into the sunset with another vendor, one who had a more accurate service quality measurement system than "tell 'ol Bill."

Too often when companies do measure service quality, they measure what is obvious...to them. To the customers, it may be some seemingly insignificant detail that makes or breaks the relationship.

Details. It's the details.

If details are important, then it is critical to get customer's input into

the design of the survey system. Let the customer tell you what is important enough to measure.

Service quality is more than a matter of doing one or two things excep-
tionally well. It is all the little stuff that wraps itself around the transaction.

3

WHY AND HOW

The company that truly understands the customer has a competitive advantage. Knowing the customer is the first step toward creating small but important points of difference. The Men's Wearhouse will press your suit for free if you purchased it from them. Probably they would press anyone's britches knowing that it is such a cheap way to build loyalty.

I buy from them. Why? Well, at least one reason is that I travel a lot and I know that if there was ever a pressing emergency, I could count on them to take up the slack.

I've never used that service but it's just one more reason. Somebody at Men's Wearhouse knows customers.

Ask your customer to tell you how you compare. Discover what is the standard and then beat it...just a little, but beat it.

In our small restaurant we had a policy that employees would eat free. Most places charge their employees half-price and blow a big horn about the wonderful benefit. Well, the truth is, restaurant folks, like the rest of us, live from paycheck to paycheck.

We didn't think it was conscionable to have a hungry employee who didn't have two nickels to rub together, come Thursday night, to be standing around mounds of hot, fresh food while his stomach rumbled. And why encourage a hungry employee to steal? We let our employees eat free. Now, we certainly didn't pay any more than our competition but you never saw a Help Wanted sign over our door.

Little differences make big differences. Ask your customer and find out what is truly important. Ask them and they will tell you how to stand out.

Remember that all of this is necessary to leadership because leadership must assemble, train, manage and lead a team to a very specific goal. Until you have your eye firmly fixed on the target, it makes little sense to shoot. Great leaders leading effective teams have done their homework. They know their customers, both traditional and internal. And measurement systems give them the industrial intelligence they need to do the job.

INDUSTRIAL SLEUTHING

The next step is to find out what you already know or could easily know. I've always been amazed over the things that the bean counters could tell you if they were so inclined or threatened. Then there is the flip side. Some times you will run into an MIS department that can't resist showing off every arcane data tidbit imaginable, choking communications in a flood of mostly useless data and nonsensical analysis.

Choose your ground. Ask. And if you don't receive, ask again. Ask until the dog wags the tail. Bean counters would often rather deliver an elegantly formatted report that is aesthetically pleasing as to hand over a mishmash of really useful information.

Chances are there is a wealth of data already being collected in your organization that could offer considerable insight if only someone would put it to work. But if collecting useless data is a national disease, failing to utilize the truly useful data already at hand, is an epidemic.

For example, what could you learn through analysis of sales by day and hour? What could you infer if you guess-timated the daily and hourly sales trends of your competition?

Home Depot, the great home-center operation, is about to begin an experiment with food operations in its larger stores as has Kmart, Target and a score of supermarket chains. This comes from the rather unremarkable observation that hourly sales spike around lunch and dinner and the supposition that perhaps folks might linger longer and buy more if they didn't have to rush out to eat.

In our hometown, retailers in the home-center business took forever to realize that they weren't just losing sales to the big discounters, they were actually sending business their way! They had the nasty habit of closing just after lunch on Saturday and remaining closed on Sunday. And just when do you think that I and the rest of humanity have time to do our home repair and fix-it projects? About the same time that they were locking their doors, we're looking for the right size nail or screw. We had no choice other than to forget it or run to the big boys who were open and waiting to take our bucks!

How much scientific analysis would it have taken to come to this great realization?

Just yesterday I visited with the operator of a major retail and catalogue sales outlet. The manager told me that he averaged over *ten–thousand* customers per day and that many are surprised to learn about their catalogue offering. Many, he said, take home a copy and place orders later.

How difficult would it be to collect the names of those who pick up a catalogue and send them a special offer a few weeks after they return home? And what about the folks who already purchase via catalogue? Couldn't their buying patterns be analyzed with the thought that they would be targets of special offers custom-tailored to their interests?

Friends in the concession industry have great problems overcoming a phenomenon called "blow by." This is what happens when patrons enter the theater and blow straight by the concession stand without taking time to purchase. Our simple research discovered that the vast majority of movie goers make going to dinner a part of the evening's experience.

Couldn't theater operators create snacks that would compliment dinner instead of spoiling it? Whatever the answer, you can't respond to a problem or opportunity you don't know exists.

What employees hate is being held accountable for something totally beyond their control. Imagine a theater operator measuring the percentage of blow by and holding concession employees accountable for selling snacks to patrons who have just eaten a big meal. Imagine a theater operator running a sales contest for popcorn the week after the FDA announced that popcorn kills from a distance!

PROCESS STEPS

Determine baseline.
Find out what you already know...or could easily know.
Determine objectives.
   Reward performance.
   Discover opportunities to improve performance.
   Discover opportunities to improve the system.
Create the survey system.
Choose measures that target the objectives.

Are the measures actionable?

Choose measurement media.

Who will be surveyed?

Create the instrument or vehicle.

Ask customers to make "trade-offs."

Encourage response.

Test for "what ifs" that could shape results.

Put the system to test, then to work.

Use rank and score to survey.

Determine weights.

Watch for minimum expectations. (Don't confuse eliminators with determinants.)

Analyze data.

Would a composite measure be valuable?

Evaluate the process.

Provide training.

Pro-active.

Remedial.

Post results.

Provide feedback to participants.

MORE PROCESS

Management sometimes forces, through insistence on following a set procedure or process, the production and delivery of inferior product and quality. Red tape, fatigue due to overwork, understaffing and other system-imposed handicaps push the crew to present to the customer less than perfect quality.

Sometimes the customer is an impediment to quality...as we see it. Customers who insist on rush jobs, who aren't satisfied until they have negotiated every last cent of potential profit out of the price and who are unclear about their requests are tremendous obstacles to quality.

Business leaders must decide if that is the way they want to do things. Some folks have a made a living out of being the schlock operator. That is a targeted strategy for them. For others, it comes naturally.

Now that you are aware, you have a special responsibility. It's up to you now to decide if you want to be all things to all people, including the bottom feeding customers in your market. Just be aware that catering to the bottom can't help but to whack off a good chunk from the top.

COMPLAINTS

Some businesses engineer the entire service quality experience based solely on customer complaints. Not a good plan.

Monitoring complaints has a valid business objective that is more than simply fixing problems; it is salvaging individual customers. In fact, research by the U.S. Department of Commerce found that customers who have had complaints that were satisfactorily resolved are more loyal than customers who have never had a reason to complain. I guess that's because once they have experienced your concern for solving their problem, they are more confident than ever that you intend to keep your service quality promise.

Ninety-five percent of customers with a complaint will return if the complaint is fixed on the spot. That is true for seven-out-of-ten complainers whose complaint is discovered after the sale. (Notice, please, that while catching and curing complaints can make a huge positive difference, it's still not quite as good as doing things right the first time around.)

Speaking of that 95 percent number, if you think that pleasing 95 percent of your customers is a great batting average, consider that on a thousand customers per week you have managed to create fifty unhappy campers who are all too eager to tell the world just how awful their experience really was. Over the course of a year, you have managed to create a small army of over *two thousand* word-of-mouth marketers for the competition.

Complaints are so powerful, either working for you or not, that every business with high customer contact should have an "At-Risk Customer" program. These are all individuals who have proven sales potential. They know your business, your people and your product. It is cheaper to woo them back into the fold than to look for a replacement. This is especially true if you consider the potential damage that could be coming due to negative word-of-mouth.

Complaints should get top priority.

And a rating of "OK" should be considered to read A-W-F-U-L!

MAKE IT EASY...

Smart businesses make it easy to complain. Try as they may, just going away never to return is even easier. Besides when conversation is at a lull at a dinner party, what better thing to talk about than those awful people over at...?

The easier it is to complain, the more likely that you will hear complaints. But better that you hear them than to hear about them. As one manager put it, "no news is bad news you haven't heard."

In the hospitality industry, 96 percent of customers with a complaint just go away. That translates to "For every complaint you hear, twenty-four customers simply left unhappy." At that rate, how many complaints can your business stand to hear...or not hear?

What could you do to make it easy to complain? An 800–number? A customer-service desk? A comment card?

Whatever you do, the response should:

> ➤ Be high-level...Let's hear from the top dog to tell me that you take this seriously.
> ➤ Extend an offer...Tell me what you are going to do to make it not just-right but better.
> ➤ Apologize...Who cares if you are right or wrong?
> ➤ Be immediate...The longer you delay, the tougher it is for me to believe that you care.

I have never been so impressed as I was after complaining to the nice folks at Shepler's Western Wear. The transgression was slight, but I wrote a letter to the president. I had no expectations, but I did want a response. What a surprise to hear from my office that the president had called looking for me. When he learned that I would return the next day, he asked if I was an early starter. Told that I was, my phone rang at 7:30 the next morning.

There was the boss, letting me know that my business was important, apologizing and offering a plan to make it better. I even received a wonderful note from the store manager. Talk about service, there it was. And I can tell you this...I shop at Shepler's and you should, too!

(By the way, in case you are wondering, I never play the "I'm an author and I write about customer service" routine. I think that's a cheap approach. Besides, I'd rather see their true colors.)

SOLID GOAL

If you aren't willing to determine right up front what you hope to accomplish with your measuring and be extremely thorough in your research, it's better leave it alone.

What sorts of goals would be reasonable to expect from measuring performance? Anything, so long as it is controllable by the performers.

You could decide that cutting service-time 15 percent would be a good goal or even increasing sales by 20 percent. You could determine that reducing employee grievances by 10 percent or improving retention by 30 percent would be good goals. Any of those are just fine as long as you keep in mind that you can't measure everything. When you try to measure everything, nothing will seem important.

Most people can handle five or six measurements on a regular basis but it's much more effective to focus on one or two. Choose speed of service or percentage of orders that are accurately filled. Then switch to another area even if you have yet to achieve your ideal in the areas you are currently measuring.

Think about measuring the ratio of complaints to transactions and when that area shows significant improvement, perhaps it's time to focus on sales per transaction.

What is most important about the process is that team players know what it takes to declare a winner. If you can only read one more management book, read my friend Chuck Coonradt's book, *The Game of Work.* Coonradt says that if there is no way to know when you are winning, you can't possibly play the game to win. You can only play and maybe not that.

People need to know what is the goal. Coonradt says that one reason that folks will work so hard at playing games is that the goal is always in sight. That's definitely not the case with 99.9 percent of jobs. Who knows what is the goal? About half the time even the boss has no idea whether or not the team is winning. So imagine what would happen to team play if not only did the players know the goal but the goal was a big, fat important one!

Link performance to a really important...call it "exciting" goal and get back, Jack!

4

BASELINE

Perhaps the best reason to create a measurement system is to find out where you are right now. This measurement is called a "baseline" measurement. This simplest of all baseline measurements is discovering that you don't have enough cash to make payroll. If that's where you are at the moment, you are reading this on behalf of your next employer!

Baseline measurements are often useful when compared to known industry standards. But be careful. If you are the best player in an industry that's going down the tubes, it's still too early to celebrate. In fact, industry standards, the so-called benchmark, could easily lead you to accept, even gloat over, performance that would be a joke in other quarters.

Remember, you are not the only one who is comparing your service against the benchmark. And the biggest threat of all is that your customers are definitely comparing your performance not with that of others in your business but with the best service providers they encounter.

Airline food always gets a bad rap without necessarily being bad food...under the circumstance. Delta served me a great breakfast of raisin bagel and cold cereal just this morning. I was perfectly satisfied to have something that was light, healthy, easily served and consumed on a relatively short flight. But the idiot in front of me couldn't get it through his skull why the attendant couldn't create a western omelette out of thin air! Delta, dude...not Lenny's!

Even something as simple as cold drinks can be a major problem in a speeding jet. Yet passengers forget that they are not sitting in the lounge at the Biltmore. They're at thirty-thousand feet being served by flight attendants who are neither equipped nor tipped to provide elegant service. They have a hundred folks to serve in a matter of minutes in an environment where something as mundane as collecting the trash is a major deal.

Reasonable or not, airline food service faces the same harsh scrutiny that would be fairly saved for a fine dining operation. The same applies no matter what product or service you provide. Customers are not comparing you with the industry standard, they are holding you to whatever standards they are used to elsewhere in their lives.

So what does the smart operator do? Start with a little competive analysis and don't confine your research to your own industry.

Mystery-shop your competitor. The big boys do. So should you.

Not a day goes by that someone from Kmart isn't prowling the aisles of Wal-Mart. And you can bet that the folks at Home Depot are watching every move at Builders Square.

You should be a regular visitor, if not customer, at your competitor's place. They should know you by name!

But don't forget to carry your micro-recorder and decoder ring when you go about the business of daily living. See how folks in other industries solve problems that may be similar to those experienced in your industry. Airlines taught banks to use serpentine lines. Too bad McDonald's hasn't taught them all just to give faster service!

Sleuthing for ideas in other industries carries the fancy name of "parallel analysis." You can call it "heads up thinking."

Keep in mind that all of this poking around is simply to find out what your customer "accepts" as good performance in your industry. You could easily be fooled, especially if your industry is already behind the times. All you'll really find out is what kind of performance is the best...of the worst. Be careful!

And, there's always that old standby technique...asking. Be careful! It's easy to come up with a number based on what customers expect from your industry even though in their heart of hearts, they are thinking about the great service they are getting elsewhere.

One fooler in the establishment of the baseline can be the trends that, although they are hard at work, are not readily revealed by today's numbers. If you look at the trends in whatever you are attempting to measure, you may come to a much different conclusion or at least set a much more realistic goal than if you simply take an average and try to beat it.

For example, if you have been losing sales at the rate of 5 percent per month, the percentage is much more ominous as a long-term trend than when viewed on a monthly basis. And if you are dealing with sales that have a natural seasonality, the actual sales figures are meaningless unless considered in the context of not just what the raw numbers are, but also in terms of what sales are actually expected. If the spring sales are normally one-hundred thousand per month and summer sales usually take a 20 percent jump, setting up a measuring system based solely on a three-month average is absolutely useless.

Once you have established your baseline performance, you are ready to get serious. The first pass at a baseline, even a third round of surveying, may be necessary before you can finally pinpoint the exact types of performance behaviors you want to measure. When you are absolutely certain that you know what your customers value, when an interpretation of your P&L has led you to the areas where improvement will do the most good, you are ready to take the next step — deciding what should be the ultimate goal of your measurement activity.

If the goal is not to improve the customer experience or get control over costs or processes that impact profitability, you simply have no reason to start.

MEASUREMENT MEDIA

Good science always takes into account the fact that it is impossible to directly measure a system without influencing the system. But heck, that takes rocket science to figure!

Stand in front of a fast-food restaurant while holding a stop watch and see what happens to service speed. You don't even need a stopwatch to see the show. In my own restaurant, I would often stand near the drive-through pressing the buttons on my pocket calculator, staring at the display as if it calculated elapsed time. To the employees inside, all that really mattered was that someone was watching.

When our franchise rep would visit and pull the same stunt, although he used a real stopwatch, regular customers would notice. Often they would comment, "I see the company guy is in town. Service was so fast, I felt like I was thrown over the hood of my car and frisked!"

I seem to remember that the phenomenon when applied to human behavior is called the Hawthorne Effect. As I recall, the name comes from job process-engineering done at a plant in Hawthorne, Calif., sometime in the year before dirt.

Every time the researchers changed something in the environment, pro-ductivity improved. They added light on the assembly line. Productivity improved. They painted the break room and got a similar result.

Ah ha! Adding light and paint improves productivity. Then someone got the dark idea to remove some of the light that had been added and guess what? Productivity improved.

Point? Any time you mess with the system, as long as it amounts to paying attention to it, things will change and probably for the better. So, don't think that just because you've installed a customer satisfaction sys-tem and things improved, that it was solely due to brilliance. It could be that for the first time, someone is actually paying attention to the things that pay the bills!

PEN OR E-MAIL?

We just received a copy of our favorite magazine and discovered that a fax-back survey was printed on the last page, bringing home the point that feedback can come in many forms. Most of us think "survey" and automatically respond with a paper-and-pen questionnaire.

Our friends at Builders Square have devised an ingenious customer survey device, a computer-based installation that sits by the exit, inviting customers to give instant response to the service they received. The sur-vey consists of key questions about knowledgeable staff, availability of product, and feelings about prices plus a few others. It can be completed in a matter of seconds using touch-screen technology.

Other clever performance feedback systems are those incorporated in the computer-based call management systems that are found wherever people spend their lives answering telephones to accept product orders, inquiries or make hotel or travel reservations. These systems tend to be largely punitive, tracking time of call and average sale per call without giving any consideration whatsoever to the quality of service as perceived by the customer.

Of course, there are the simple count-'em-as-they-are-stamped-out sys-tems built into many manufacturing operations. They work just fine for measuring quantity. But quality is something all together different. Be-sides, it's the total experience we wrap around the transaction that regis-ters with the customer, not just the product itself.

One feedback system that's hard to beat is the tried-and-true practice of simply asking. Actually, there is nothing simple about asking custom-ers to tell us about their experience. When you walk out of a restaurant, what is the most likely phrase you will hear? It's, "Was everything alright?" You hear that repeatedly. And what do you say, whether the food and service was world-class or a double-over-toss-your-cookie-platter?

"Fine."

Yeh, right! Fine.

Well, is that "fine" as in "that's the best meal I ever put in my mouth," or "fine" as in "If I live to eat again, may the Lord strike me dead if I darken your door"?

Customers who don't feel comfortable talking to you certainly aren't going to make a scene telling you how to improve your business. You've got to get out and mingle. Establish a relationship. Earn the right to hear the bad news in full gory detail not just a whimpered "fine" as they skulk out the door.

Look Who's Calling After Dinner

Some customers have little or nothing to say. They're happy with you, your product and it hasn't even crossed their mind that you might want to hear their opinion. Some customers wouldn't be happy if you gave them the business and offered to run it for them!

And some employees don't particularly want to know what customers have to say. Use a customer feedback system to determine compensation and you invite employees to stack the deck or do whatever it takes to shape results. So what is the best way to find out what customers really think?

One very good way is to telephone customers at random. This avoids the ugly fact that customers most likely to complete a comment card are those who have a complaint. By telephoning you get to hear the good, the bad and the totally ambivalent. And customers are often absolutely blown away by the simple fact that you asked.

Pick customers at random. Think before you call.

One restaurateur friend does this but only calls customers who visited with a large group.

He made that decision after mistakenly calling a guest who was definitely not supposed to be dining with company. At least that was the cleaned-up version he heard from the angry spouse who answered the phone!

Sample

Still on the table is the matter of sample size and composition. There are statistical rules that should be followed if your survey is also a project for a degree program. Otherwise use common sense and you'll be fine. If you decide to call or otherwise sample 1 percent, a number that may not be statistically significant, and you get a consistent response, that's plenty.

The question is not so much a matter of how many folks you survey but what you do with the information that they share. better than sampling more is doing more.

Who do you sample?

As Frank Felicella, CEO of Builders Square likes to say, "sample some with bags...and some without."

Small point but packed with insight.

Asking customers who purchase is fine for finding out how you can please customers who are already at least at the "satisfied enough to come in" level. But what about those who came in and didn't buy? And those folks who never darkened the door? "Some with bags, some without."

Smart leaders want to know the why behind lack of trial or trial that didn't produce a sale.

Don't forget to measure how much of your product and service your customers are buying. You've heard it a gazillion times. A server approaches your table and suggests dessert. A salesclerk brings out a tie that matches the new suit perfectly. A travel planner offers a discount for extending your stay. Even the dentist shows you the latest in cosmetic technique. All of this is to get you, the customer, to buy more.

And why not? You're there! They don't have to go looking for another customer. Why should they? They have one at the table, in the dressing room, on the phone, strapped to the chair! (My dentist straps me to the chair. That is the way it's supposed to be done, isn't it?)

Time out for a reminder that all of this applies to both sides of the salesbook. What about the really great team players who never showed up for try outs? What about those who tried out but didn't sign? What about those who are now playing for the competition?

We think, sometimes to do exit interviews when key employees leave for greener pastures. But how often do we give an exit interview to discover, really discover, why someone declined a perfectly good job offer? And when was the last time you asked a potential player why they didn't apply to play on your team?

Hiring a team of winners is a marketing effort as certain as is the recruitment of customers. There is always a reason why good people play for the competition. Find out what those reasons are and position your team as **the** team.

Scott's Law Of Expansion:
A business will expand to accommodate
the number of winning team players it hires.

Hire all the winners. Get all the business.

5

TRY IT...YOU MIGHT HATE IT!

You might even consider experiencing your own service just to see how it feels. A friend who used to work for a Singapore-based company told me how the employees of his firm revolted over the prospects of flying their national airline, British Airlines. They simply refused to travel BA which was the company airline by policy.

When they began to hear from other travelers that BA had changed, they decided to give it a try and were pleasantly surprised to be pleasantly surprised. It seems that the chairman of the airline, tired of being accosted by friends and relatives with horror stories, decided that the quickest fix could be engineered by requiring top executives to experience their own airline from the cattle crush of the economy section rather than from the cushy comfort of first class.

When you try to survey customers in person, you trade the precise measurement of the formal questionnaire for the vagaries of conversation. If you are observant and articulate, your chances of discovering meaningful information increase considerably. That's because as people answer your questions, they tend to drop verbal clues about their unspoken feelings.

To unearth true feelings, avoid questions that tend to cutoff further comment.

"How was everything?" nearly begs the customer to say "Fine."

"How did we do today?" is better but not by much.

"Did you find everything you were looking for and were we able to help you?" is closer yet.

But, "What could we do to make your next visit even better?" is a question that would seem left unanswered by a whispered, "Nothing."

CUSTOMER-EYES IDEAS

➤ Is this your first visit?
➤ Where else do you like to shop? Dine? Purchase computers?
➤ Are we doing things the way you like?
➤ What would you change?
➤ What do you like best?
➤ Do we do any little things that bug you?
➤ Do you recommend us to your friends?
➤ How could we do better next time?
➤ How often do you do business with us?
➤ How much of your _____ business do you do with us?
➤ What could we do to get all of your _____ business?

Good managers are perpetually asking.

They ask customers and players alike for their input knowing full well that not only is the phrase, "the more you ask, the more you learn," true but so is "the more often you ask, the more likely they will think you really want to hear."

While imprisoned in our local hospital following an emergency appendectomy, a young woman knocked on my door and asked if I had time for a survey.

"Time! All I seem to have is time. Come in."

"We're doing a survey for the food-service department. Was your food served at the right temperature?"

"Yes."

"Was the selection satisfactory?"

"Yes."

"Was it served on time and was your order accurate?"

"Yes to both."

"Were you able to chew it?"

"I'm here for an appendectomy not gum surgery."

"Thank you!"

"Wait just a minute. Don't you want to know how it tasted?"

"No, sir. That's not on my questionnaire."

"Well, it is now. If I had been color blind and couldn't tell the red food from the green food, I would not have been able to tell what any of it was much less formed an expectation of how it should taste. Haven't you noticed how many fast-food joints are delivering here?"

"I'm sorry, sir. That's not on my form."

CONSEQUENCES...

Measurement systems are often perceived as punishment and sometimes they both are and should be.

We had a one-time client who asked us to help improve customer service and, hopefully as a consequence, their sales. Right away we realized that they didn't want us to succeed. Their founder had ordered our hiring and it quickly became apparent that the executive group that we were working with wouldn't be receptive to any recommendations for change.

So why hire us? They wanted us to add a blessing to their current practices or at the very least refrain from making recommendatons that were so different from the norm that it would make them look incompetent.

They had a right to be worried.

Immediately we asked a few key questions about how folks were compensated, whether or not service was measured and what ideas they had as explanation to poor sales performance.

This company was famous for tight controls over inventory. They had an elaborate system that polled stores every night and immediately notified management if inventory and cash failed to balance.

Unfortunately, in spite of all this supposed sophistication, there was no link between the cash register and the inventory unit. Sales were whatever the manager reported.

Worse, store management had been told that they absolutely had to spend 6 percent of sales on free samples.

We visited more than a dozen of their stores in three markets and never once saw any evidence of sampling even though the managers reported, you guessed it, an even 6 percent of product missing from inventory due to sampling.

Got any idea where the product went?

My guess, heh, heh, is that it was sold and the buckos formed a powerful disincentive to support any system that measured performance if it involved feedback from customers who had received samples. Why? Because there weren't any!

So the top executives did everything they could to keep us from creating feedback systems. They didn't want to face their mercurial founder with the news that there was mass theft nor did they want to deal with the inevitable negative reaction from store managers losing 6 percent of their take home.

So, like it or not, you had better include in your thinking a mental investigation in search of those who may have a vested interest that isn't 100 percent in sync with that of the organization.

GETTING INPUT

One problem that is part and parcel to changing the system by measuring it, is the problem of getting customers to participate. Sometimes customers can become upset with a system that to them seemed to be working just fine simply because we imposed on them by asking for assistance in the measurement.

We do all of our travel-related business with Carlson. At least that's what they think. Actually, we do business with Nancy and crew who just happen to work for Carlson. Every now and again, they enclose a customer service survey form with our tickets. I'm busy. I don't have time to fill out a form every time I turn around. And I'm a nice guy! So, if I feel that way, imagine how some folks must feel. It's probably "no" followed by "hell, no!"

Actually, I fill mine out saying that I'm really Nancy's customer and that "...if she goes, I go. So take care of Nancy!"

The simple fact is, many if not most customers just aren't interested in managing your business for you. If you want their help, you had better answer that age-old-question...WIIFM. What's in it for me?

Here's a lesson straight out of Positively Outrageous Service. Rather than offering every respondent some small token of appreciation for their participation, offer them a chance to join the other respondents in a drawing for something really spectacular. For example, a hotel chain might offer a chance to win a weekend for two. A clothier might offer to draw for a complete business wardrobe. Whatever the deal, it will be less expensive overall than giving everyone something small.

Or try offering something personal. We survey our speaking clients with the promise that one lucky respondent will receive a tin of Melanie's "world famous or should be" holiday baked goods.

Another big problem occurs when the number of questions you would like to have answered, results in a questionnaire that is so lengthy that it becomes an imposition. Solution? Simple! Break the list into smaller, more manageable parts and ask customers only one part of the list. Rotate the smaller lists of questions knowing that even though no one customer answered all of the questions, because you spread the chore over a larger pool, statistically the results are identical.

No, better, because asking a customer to answer a long and cumbersome questionnaire is likely to illicit testy responses that pull the satisfaction curve downward.

As long as we're on the subject, a good rule of thumb is to limit customer survey input to about two minutes. Beyond that, they start to skew the responses toward, "Don't bother me."

Ask questions that could be answered "yes" or "no" but offer a range of response choices on an easily understandable scale. Leave room for free-hand comments so that you don't shut yourself out of an important comment simply because you failed to ask.

Always include room for name, address and phone number. If there's a serious complaint, you'll need that information.

Whatever you do, don't make comment cards a part of the reward system. The deck will be perceived as "stacked" even when it isn't...but it will be.

One unexpected source of customer feedback is performance evaluations. This is not a suggestion for either the impatient, the immature or the fainthearted. But at least consider what has come to be known as 360-degree evaluations. Three-sixties involve team players being evaluated by their leaders, their peers and their subordinates. When it's the leader's turn in the box, those that she has been charged to serve get to report how well the leader has served.

Where work is done by teams, (isn't that everywhere?) team players are also evaluated on their contribution to the team and their performance as a member of the team. Did they contribute? Were they on time to meetings and with their work? Did they get along with their teammates and did they play as a team member or as a lone hot dog out for glory?

This is all a matter of listening to the customer — this time, the internal customer.

6

RANK AND SCORE

Poorly constructed surveys can often do more harm than good particularly when they lead to conclusions that may be off-base even though they are accurate. Impossible to be both? Not at all!

A Chicago hotel marketing executive surveyed guests and discovered that nearly 100 percent wanted a television in the bathroom. Presented with the survey results, the sharp general manager had the foresight to ask how the question was constructed. It turned out that guests had simply been asked if they would enjoy having a television in the bathroom. And who wouldn't?

On further surveying, reality returned to focus when guests were asked less directed questions such as...please list the amenities you most appreciate in a hotel room and rank them according to their importance to you. The overwhelming, surprising, and considerably cheaper-to-fulfill request was for an iron and ironing board.

Point: Not everything is equally important to the customer. Why construct a survey that assumes just the opposite?

A great technique is to ask respondents to rank an item according to its relative importance and give a score according to how well that need is currently being met. For example, customers of an auto body shop might rank having a clean waiting area as being very important yet give the business a very low score. This would be a definite call to action.

On the other hand, they might list that having free fresh-brewed coffee is not important to them while rating the quality of the vending machine coffee available as very low. In this case, it's a "so what?" when other more important factors are considered.

Using composite scores based on the combined average of weighted subscores gives the measurement fairness and stability. With composite scores, a single out of line subscore is much less likely to skew the composite total unfairly or perhaps better said, "unreasonably."

One problem that is tough to avoid is this issue of "weight." Even though asking for a rank and score for each attribute tends to lessen the potential for misinterpretation, it's a good idea to ask the customer for an overall score. When it comes to giving an overall score, possible confusion over terms and attributes gives way to plain old feelings.

When you think about it, it is always the customer's mental composite score, the sum of a jillion big and little transgressions and treats, that causes them to turn into your parking lot or keep on driving.

If you are going to use the system to determine wage increases and as part of the basis for promotion decisions, do this:

1) Measure something the performer can control;
2) Measure a reasonable number of attributes that really matter;
3) Assign attributes an appropriate weight based on customer perception; and
4) Use a composite score from a fair sample.

Be certain to make your measurements inflation-proof. Use "units" rather than dollars, for example. Begin by establishing a baseline measure such as absenteeism on Fridays that has been calculated over a long enough period to make the number reliable.

One additional pitfall is getting confused over expectations. For example, surveys show that safety is very important to airline passengers yet it is listed as a minor element when customers actually make the decision about which airline to fly. Why? Because all airlines are safe. That an airline will be safe is taken as a given. The only time safety would be a serious consideration in the purchase decision would be if an airline was perceived to be **un**safe.

There are many factors that contribute to the perception of service quality. Some are positive but not important. Some are negative but not sufficiently so to direct the customer elsewhere. Some factors are "determinant factors," attributes that shape purchase behavior in a major way. Airline safety is not by its presence a determinant factor, only by its absence.

Whatever the results, they can be evaluated in terms of rank and score.

Rank is the relative importance and score is a measurement of how well that need is being met.

We Hold These Truths to Be...

You're waiting for me to write, "self-evident." Sorry. The truth is that while all customers may have been created equally, they for darned sure aren't equal at the cash register. Now before you misinterpret that, all I am saying is that not all customers have the same value to the business.

Smart managers teach their employees about the value not of "customers," but of "customer." This is a subtle yet important distinction.

Not all customers are equal in terms of sales potential or referral possibilities. A customer who only shops when something is "on deal" just can't be worth as much as a regular, full-fee paying customer. Some customers have value beyond the amount that you can run through the cash register. These customers are called "influentials." Their value lies not just in what they spend but in what they can or could influence others to spend.

You remember an "influential" from high school, someone who always was first not to follow a trend but first to start a trend. In sixth grade I was given a bright red beret. Just the thing for a snot-nosed kid in small town Kentucky. On some kids that would be an invitation to get punched out. For me, it was enough to inspire several other sixth graders to scarf up berets of their own. Then, of course, a few seventh graders decided to commence punching.

You may not have thought of it, especially if you have a small business where every customer is dear, but...not all customers are good for your business. A large customer that ties up most of your resources may, in the long run, hinder growth. A large customer that requires all of your energy could keep you from fully developing your potential market. Think how you will feel the day that some other little guy underbids you simply to claim the giant on their resume.

Not all customers fit the organization.

This is as true for employees who, although they may bring to the party incredible expertise, may not be the kind of player your company can afford culturally, let alone financially.

But the point remains, that some customers are more valuable than others. Smart managers admit that to themselves and teach their teams to recognize the difference.

On a related thought, if all customers are not equal, why should their input into a service quality measurement system be treated equally? Think about it.

WHAT TO ASK

What you ask depends somewhat upon whom you are asking although there is a surprising similarity between survey questions for internal and traditional customers. You may need to tweak the wording but often not much more.

You could ask traditional customers, "Do you recommend us to your friends?" Ask internal customers the exact same question.

Ask traditional customers, "Do you buy our full line?" Ask internal customers if they participate fully in company events and programs.

Ask traditional customers if they intend to purchase again in the near future. Ask internal customers if they see a future working with you.

Whatever questions that you ask, look for intentions and behavior rather than attitude. An employee or customer may tell you one thing and do something entirely different. It is the behavior that really counts.

Here is a set of questions that work either way:

➤ Who are our competitors?
➤ How do we compare with the competition?
➤ What new products or services do they have that appeal to you?

Think for a moment about just how competitive things are, not just for customers, but for team players as well.

CAN WE TALK?

Your actions are speaking so loudly, I can't hear what you are saying.

I don't remember where I heard that but it describes your business, and mine, to a T.

We tell employees that quality counts and then say, "That's good enough." We talk about being fanatics about quality and ask our employees to work in a dark, dilapidated office. We talk, all right, but what are we really saying?

The messages that we send our customers by far transcend the canned greeting that we force employees to deliver. We spend for a fifty-foot lighted pole sign but fail to pull the weeds from around the parking area. Get it? Everything we say and do, the way we look and maintain our equipment is sending a giant message to our customers.

Think for a moment about the various communications we send.

The way we answer the telephone.

The look of our mail.

Our building exterior.

Our personal appearance including our habits.

Our commercials, product demos, packaging and logos.

Everything we say or do or allow to be said on our behalf, adds up to...us.

Step back. Way back. Approach your business the way a customer approaches it. Start in the Yellow Pages. Drive in from a different direction. Call the receptionist. Complain to Customer Service. Call and ask if you are accepting applications. Have lunch in the employee break room. Try the employee john. Live for a week on the average employee salary. See how you like it.

Take a good, hard, long look and hear what you see.

Maybe you won't need a fancy service quality measurement system for a while. There may be plenty of the obvious that needs attention.

WHAT TO DO WITH THE RESULTS

What everyone seems to like to do with service quality measurement systems is to use them to hit people over the head. Not a good idea just a common one.

But you can use them to determine at least part of an employee's compensation. This is especially useful where employee performance is difficult to quantify in terms of dollar impact on the bottom line.

For example, let's say that an employee is a customer service representative. There may be no products to sell, no services that can be billed. But surely a pleasant, efficient customer service rep has a positive impact on sales and profits. Why not make customer feelings about how well they were handled as part of the bonus or salary system?

Be certain to let the customers set the standards.

You'd be surprised what you could decide based purely on service quality measurement. You might decide to raise the spending authority of your mid-level clerks. You could decide that since all customers have different needs, they should be surveyed for individual preferences. You could even learn that the magazines in the waiting area need to be retargeted. Ask and ye shall, you know what!

What you don't want to do is focus on the area that gets the lowest score. That could easily have you working on something that is urgent...just not at all important. Spend your attention working on things that count, really count.

Besides, low scores, all by themselves, could mean anything including, customers don't care about the attribute being measured, they have low expectations that are being met, no one in your industry does any better, or they just plain didn't get the question. Look before you leap.

You could easily ignore low expectations but why? If the entire industry does a poor job in one area, you are looking at a solid gold opportunity. Imagine an auto salvage yard that was clean, a dry cleaner that didn't crush buttons, a bus station with clean restrooms, a garage without grease on the floor, a doctor that didn't make you wait, a government agency that treated you like the paying customer you are.

When the results are in, make certain that the performer gets them immediately. Don't let them languish on the desk of some manager who doesn't have actual hands-on responsibility. Service quality measurement systems do not, by themselves, guarantee a change. They have to be put to work.

A recent survey by Bain and Company and the Planning Forum reported in *Fortune* magazine that having the latest management tools was no indicator of success. Although 94 percent of the companies surveyed had mission statements, 90 percent did customer surveys and 76 percent practiced TQM, there was no correlation between having the tools and profitability. You've got to do something!

For the measurement system to be taken seriously, it must be used to influence future raises and assignments. However, it should not be the sole determinant. When it is used, it should be current performance compared to baseline. Otherwise it's quite possible that a company that is doing well, could end up rewarding poor performance. And a poorly performing company could end up punishing good performers, losing them before they are able to make a difference.

ACT ON PERFORMANCE...
DON'T REACT TO PERFORMERS

One big question is, "What if our measurement system indicates that our people really aren't performing anywhere close to standard?"

You must be prepared to provide the feedback and assistance that is needed to improve performance. But...here's the catch...you must do it in a way that is not a threat. The time to make these decisions is before you begin a service quality measurement program. It is important to position additional training as a benefit, not a punishment.

Having the boss single you out for additional training is like being sent to the slow reader group in elementary school. You know and everybody else knows and you know that everybody knows that no matter what color or animal they name the group after, you're still going to the dummy group. And it never feels pretty.

You can ease the pain by announcing right up front that the goal is to get better and that team members who participate fully in additional training are team players who put the team first and deserve applause for their effort.

There is one further issue at hand, the issue of privacy. The Privacy Act was written with the intention that individuals not be subjected to embarrassment through the unnecessary publication of their performance. A nice idea but, hey! Who doesn't already know which team members are contributing and which are not? Still, there is no point in rubbing salt. In fact, it can be downright counterproductive.

If you were to post individual performance scores, how do you think the poorest performer would react? I'll tell you. He, or she, will immediately attempt to save face by bad-mouthing the entire system. The system will stink and those who are busting a gut are engaged in plain, old brown-nosin'. Once it is seen that there is no way to improve to reach the set standard, performance may actually get worse out of some odd sense of silent protest. "I'll never be able to hit those stupid goals. No sense in bustin' a gut trying."

Post the team results but deliver individual performance feedback in private.

PROVIDE FEEDBACK TO RESPONDENTS

One additional way to improve the quality and quantity of responses is to promise...and then deliver...feedback to the respondents. If people are reluctant to spend time completing surveys, they are doubly so when they are unlikely to be informed of the results. It's even worse when they have no reason to expect that action will be taken as a result of their effort.

As an aside, customers like to know that they can be heard, if they want to be heard.

General managers, in one division of Morrison's (Ruby Tuesday restaurants) wear beepers while on duty. Guests who have a problem or complaint can call the number listed on the table tent and beep the manager on duty for immediate resolution! Top that!

At Hershey Park in beautiful Hershey, Penn., employees who submit suggestions or complaints are invited to employee "therapy" sessions where they learn how their input has been acted upon. Thanks to the sessions, employee input has increased dramatically.

In eight years of having a restaurant with my name prominently posted on the menu, only once did a customer actually call our home to complain. I haven't the foggiest idea what he wanted. When I answered the phone and he heard the family having dinner in the background, he said, "Did this number ring into your home?"

"Yes, sir. Don't let that bother you. We're very serious about serving our guests. How can I help you?"

"Well, I guess it's not all that important."

He hung up.

Whatever you do, make certain that when a customer takes the time to respond to any kind of survey at all that they are acknowledged. A simple thank-you note will do. If you are responding to a specific complaint or they mentioned something specifically on the survey, you, too, must be specific in your reply. With modern technology, there is no excuse not to customize even form letters. In fact, a generic form letter is worse than no response at all. At least if you do not reply, there is a possibility that you did not receive my input. Reply halfheartedly and I'll **know** you just don't care. Plus, you will preclude any possibility that I will communicate in the future.

CHECKLIST!

Program is...
___Objective
___Consistent
___Reliable

Design...
___Measures performance
___Provides actionable data
___Response scales are easily understood
___Surveys a well-rounded sample; Includes long-term, new and prospective customers

___Intent is continuous but designed for change

___Method of collection produces reliable data

___Identifies customers with specific problems

___System in place for using feedback on a daily basis

___Ties to compensation and assignment plans

___Executive bonus plans are more feedback-dependent than line employees

7

Making Work Joyful

It wouldn't be right not to end this section without at least a short discussion of making work joyful. I never thought about it before myself, but it's useful to ask why some work isn't joyful and maybe flip the answers into the positive.

Here's my list on the joyfulness of work:

Joyful – Has a purpose larger than mere profit.

Awful – Product or service produced has no larger purpose.

Joyful – Has a strong connection between the work and the results.

Awful – Worker cannot see results of the effort or connect to the finished product.

Joyful – Customers are viewed as individuals.

Awful – Customers are unseen or remain nameless.

Joyful – A healthy balance exists between physical and mental efforts.

Awful – There is little or no balance between physical and mental work.

Joyful – There is variety in the work and customers.

Awful – Work and customer requests are monotonous.

Joyful – The work environment is professional yet playful.

Awful – There is no room for play in the work environment.

Joyful – There is a strong sense of ownership and pride of craft.

Awful – There is no sense of ownership or pride of craft.

Joyful – Work has a beginning and an end or at the least logical occasions for celebration.

Awful – The work seems to be unending.

There is a saying that I first heard at the National Speakers Association, "It is easier to make a buck than to make a difference." What a truth! I think back to the days when we definitely weren't making any bucks and realize now that maybe it's because we weren't really making much of a difference either.

Look at the majority of the folks who are doing well financially and you'll see not just a group of high achievers, you'll be looking at a group of high producers.

Can't you just hear that resonant voice of the fabled Earl Nightingale plugging away from the tape deck as he tells us, that "it's easier to adapt to the hardships of a poor living than to do the things necessary to live well"?

The winners in life, according to Nightingale, are those who are willing to do the things that the losers just aren't prepared to do. Choices. That's what we're talking about.

Work that is joyful is work that has as its focus some other purpose than piling bucks in the bank. Do what you love and the money will follow.

If that's so fine for the boss, why should it not be just as fine for the worker bees? Isn't it up to the boss to think about purpose beyond the profit and loss statement? Look at the truly successful business endeavor and you will see companies that make a difference in the lives of their customers and employees.

Ben and Jerry's, the ice cream gurus, help look after the rain forests. The Hershey Company provides a home, education and guidance to nearly 2,000 disadvantaged young people. Think about it. Sneaking a mouthful of Rainforest Crunch and breaking off a piece of a Kit Kat bar can actually have a noble as well as sinfully delicious purpose.

We often donate a portion of back of the room sales to the kids and families at the Ronald McDonald House as do our friends at Southwest Airlines. It is possible to do good and do well. Probably in the long run, these ideas are not mutually exclusive but perhaps mutually dependent.

What could you do to give your business a greater purpose? How could you involve your employees in the act of doing good? Or could you just help them see more clearly how what they do makes a difference in the lives of the folks they serve?

CONNECT THE DOTS

Did you ever play at one of those rainy day activity books that your Mom kept around to help you through the chicken pox? There was always a page or two of connect the dots. You remember, the page was covered with a jillion numerals in a meaningless pattern that only took on character after you drew a line from one to two and so on. Where there had only been a bunch of numbered dots, there appeared a picture.

Work is too often like a bunch of unconnected dots. You can't ever see the picture. Like the blind men struggling to describe an elephant, the boss hands you the tail and tells you that you should be happy.

How could you be happy when you can't tell if your hard work ever amounts to anything? How could a normal person be satisfied watching their work ooze along an assembly line to nowhere? People need to be able to connect the work they do today with a result. And hopefully, that result has some value that transcends the cash register.

REAL PEOPLE

The big buzz in the meeting's industry is all about the information superhighway and how it threatens to make meetings obsolete. No way. Meetings of the face-to-face variety will increase as a result of people wanting to meet the folks they have come to know via copper wire and fiber optic.

Think about who in your organization would like to visit with someone in a branch office that they may talk to on a daily basis but have yet to meet or see exactly how that office looks and where everyone sits. These are internal customers that we struggle to see as people.

Imagine how this applies to traditional customers.

What if the dry cleaner knew that the shirt she was pressing would be worn to the funeral of a loved one. Would the buttons be crushed? Would the collar lay funny?

What if the truck driver knew that the box marked "fragile" in purple crayon contained a craft project from Grandma's favorite? Would he toss it on the pile or let it be stacked on the bottom?

And what about the speaker who was about to talk to the fourth audience of the week? Would he "phone it in" because he was too tired to give it his best? Would he do that if he knew that the group had saved their entire speaker's budget just so they could hear his special words? I think not.

When employees see only the dots and not the picture, there is little reason to be surprised when they act as though their work has no meaning. To them it doesn't.

Connecting customers to the work makes all the difference. It is a prerequisite for joy on the job.

8

BALANCE, GRASSHOPPER, BALANCE

W hen I was a kid, I asked my folks if I could borrow the car to drive to Tampa. I wanted to see a girlfriend who was in town visiting her grandmother. To me, the trip was a very big deal. The drive would be about a hundred miles to a strange town in our family car (and all this only a few months after turning sixteen!)

My folks were great. Here they were trusting me with our only car and I was absolutely determined to earn that trust. To make sure that I would be okay, my dad insisted that he replace the tires before the trip.

We weren't exactly what you would call "rolling in money." So when Dad commissioned me to find four retreads and get them on the car, I understood without being told to make every penny count.

I negotiated the best deal at our local service station, but even good deals only go so far, and I, too, had to make a few concessions. Actually, I made four concessions.

I decided that new tires should not be out of balance. After all, they were "new." So I gave up balancing in favor of whitewalls, a big deal in 1966.

Damned near bounced all the way from Gainesville to Tampa. I was so glad to see Karen McKewan, I would have hugged her if I hadn't been too shy and shaking too hard to locate her.

That's the way a job can be. When it's out of balance, you never feel comfortable. You know something is wrong but you don't know what.

What is wrong is that you have too much of one thing and not enough of the other. Why did we love to watch *M*A*S*H*? Because there they were, in the middle of a horrible war, doing everything they could think of doing to put their lives back into balance. In the operating room, there was still time for humor. And Klinger sought to balance the insanity of war with a little insanity of his own.

Balance at work means that there is indeed a time to work and a time to play. There is a time to think as well as a perfectly good time to take inventory or clean the parking lot. People can't keep their mental balance when they are glued to a telephone or an assembly line or a loading dock. They need balance.

When you cross-train employees, you are doing more than establishing a line of defense against turnover or absenteeism. You are building a point of balance for your crew, an opportunity for them to break the everyday routine and bring balance to their work. It's also an opportunity to see their work environment from a different perspective, to create solutions for one job position while working in another.

PRIDE OF CRAFT

Years ago I heard a wonderful speaker-consultant by the name of Bill Oncken explain how our jobs change as we progress up the ladder. At first, said Bill, we find ourselves doing jobs that really turn us on because they give us a strong sense of identity and pride of craft. Think about the first job you had and, dollars to donuts, you'll be describing a job that, even though entry level, gave you a tremendous sense of identity and pride of craft.

Were you a paper carrier? Could you hit the porch while pedaling ninety-miles to nothin'?

Are you still proud to drive through those neighborhoods thinking of them as "your" territory?

Or maybe you were a dishwasher like me. There was no finer feeling than to mop my way to the back door at the end of the day. Just before I would turn out the lights and remove my apron to wipe up my single footprint by the breaker box, I would always steal one last look into the kitchen and swell at what seemed like a mile of glistening tile and polished stainless. Call it foolish if you like but I, T. Scott Gross, was the dishwasher. Okay, extraordinaire, if you insist.

Whatever it was, the first job that made you really excited about going to work, gave you a strong sense of identity and a pride of craft. It may not have been rocket science but, by golly, you were a pro!

How do your employees feel about their work? Do they have a little freedom of choice or must it be done in lockstep because the god of operations knows exactly how things must be done?

Walk into the nearest fast-food restaurant or department store where they are given a required greeting to lay on every customer. Tell me how much joy you hear in those voices. Well, I'll tell you that a cheerful "What's happenin', homie?" beats a dour "Welcome to ____. How may I serve you?" any day of the week.

We spoke to a retail group not long ago where some genius district manager had instructed the sales staff to answer the phone, "Thanks for calling ____ during our Jurassic sale. Have we got a dinosaur of a deal for you." Pfffftt!

How can there be joy at work where you have no control, no freedom? The job has nothing to do with your brain or your uniqueness. There you are only another nameless cog in a lifeless machine.

START, STOP, CHANGE

The Scientologists define control as the ability to start, stop or change. Not a bad definition. Think about how much or little control there is at work. What can you start, stop or change? If there is no answer that fits that question, you probably feel little joy in going to work.

What is it that turns on top executives if it isn't the ability to decide and watch someone else turn those intangible decisions into reality? And why should it be unreasonable for all of us to be able to exercise a little control at work?

Worse perhaps than being or feeling powerless on the job may be our inability to see an end, a result. It's one computation or form followed by another. One new part added to the assembly and sent bumping along the conveyor belt. One more cranky passenger with too much carry-on followed by another who is even crankier and more retentive.

The worst thing about too many jobs is that they have absolutely no beginning and no end. Just another event like the last event.

Smart managers find clever ways to mark or even create an end to things. End of project or at least end of month. Drag out a cake. Blow up a few balloons. Celebrate the millionth widget if that's what you sell. But for sanity's sake, celebrate something.

Every time we sell a custom, video-based training program or another keynote, the phone rings. Before you can get the receiver to your ear, you recognize the godawful clang of a cowbell. When the noise retreats back into the phone, a voice that belongs to Jim Chism says, "Ring the bell! We got another one!"

I've been watching his cumulative sales. By the time he reads this, he will have received a handsome brass bell engraved with the words, "First Ever Bell Ringer's Award" for reaching a sales milestone. We'll have a nice dinner, a short presentation. And then he'll excuse himself to start working on a bigger bell.

HELP! WE HAVE TO HELP!

Yesterday we visited by the pool with our friends, Al and Mary Helen DeLiberto, who I have mentioned in previous chapters run the fabulously successful Boccones restaurant in San Antonio, Texas.

In the course of conversation, Al mentioned the topic of one of his recent weekly staff meetings. It turned out that he had decided to talk at some length about the concept of cause and effect, not exactly your expected topic for a restaurant staff meeting.

But then, there isn't much that you could call ordinary or expected about this restaurant or its leadership.

Al said, "You know, the average young person today doesn't seem to have much of an understanding about the relationship between the decisions they make and the impact on their career and life. It was amazing to me that, after what seemed to me to be a bit of a fatherly kind of talk, that five of my employees came up to thank me."

I'm not certain but this may not really be a trend. In fact, I remember my father having the same kinds of talks with employees as far back as the sixties. Maybe it's just a part of growing up and maybe some folks never quite get the message. Whatever the case, it's a puzzle to me how some folks get stuck in jobs that make them miserable, working for bosses that beat them to a mental pulp. (You could wonder the same thing about abusive marriages and other relationships that aren't happy.)

In a not very good movie starring George Burns and Brooke Shields, she walks into the house owned by the character played by Burns and says, "Wow! You must be rich." Burns puffs on the omnipresent cigar and replies, "You don't must be anything. It's a choice."

It is a choice and it escapes me why people seem so hell-bent on making dumbhead choices. Maybe it's as Al said, that some folks just can't quite make the connection between the choices they make and the lives they live.

For me, I choose joy.

IN SUMMARY...

Customers who come to you for quality, and most do, never experience your organization chart. They experience the process. So process standards should reflect customer expectations. The flip side of that coin is that the organization chart should reflect the process which in turn should reflect customer expectations. It just may be that your processes are built around the organization instead of the other way around.

PART V

SHAPING

1

SELLER'S MARKET

HIRING IN A SERVICE ECONOMY

In the new economy, employees must be different. Don't jump too quickly and assume that whatever happens, it is the employee's failure to respond that is at fault. Not only must employees themselves be different, so must the way that they must be recruited, trained and managed.

What the world has failed to realize is that we are not moving toward a service economy, it's a done deal. *Fait accompli. Finito.* Got it? Service jobs account for 74 percent of the Gross Domestic Product and a full 79 percent of the jobs. (And aren't you surprised to see those numbers so close?)

I bet you expected the jobs to weigh in at some whopper of a number while their value was some teeny-weeny, embarrassment to a developed country. In a service economy, while there are a gazillion fairly low-paid burger flippers, there are also plenty of highly skilled, highly compensated cardiologists, entertainers and more attorneys than we could need in a century! Believe it or not, the median wage difference between service and manufacturing jobs amounts to a paltry nineteen dollars per week!

The idea of a manufacturing economy has been dead for decades. What didn't die (but should have) are most of our ideas about recruiting, hiring, training, managing and compensating employees. Those ideas sort of hung on for lack of awareness and a better plan.

Besides, the old ideas have been working just fine, thank you. Why bother to fix what is obviously not broken?

Obvious or not, the system is broken. The old ways no longer work. Maybe they never did.

In the hospitality industry, only the optimistic few speak in terms of employee retention. The rest of us say turnover. And why not? It's not unusual for a restaurant or hotel to have turnover in excess of 300 percent.

We laugh to hear of folks in that industry running contests that last for a full year. A year-long contest in hospitality? You've got to be kidding!

Winning those is easy. All you have to do is stay! You don't have to be good; you don't really have to perform. All you need do is to outlast the other guy!

Why? Why would there be turnover in any industry that exceeds 300 percent? For years the stock answer has been to grouse about employees who just don't want to work, who are lazy, unreliable and the list goes on. It's true. Those words fairly describe too many in the American workforce.

Do you want to know why? Because we made that kind of work/behavior possible. It is very possible to change jobs, like most folks change underwear, to steal from one employer and repeat that same behavior two blocks down the street.

When the Texas Employment Commission asked employers why they terminated employees, the near unanimous response was, "They don't come to work or if they do, they're not on time and if they are, they don't perform."

Pretty sorry state of affairs but true. Thirty-two percent of workers fired by this group lost their jobs for failure to report on time or at all. Nineteen percent lose out to "bad attitude or poor work ethic" and 18 percent are terminated for "dishonesty or failure to follow work rules."

(P.S. here...failure to follow work rules is the reason most folks give when they can't prove in a court of law that the day's receipts walked when an employee who was supposed to be making the deposit "lost" the bag or was "robbed" on the way to the bank.)

The top reasons for turning down employees reads, for the most part, like a list of failed dreams and values. According to the Texas Employment Commission, those reasons are:

Lack of experience
Inability to communicate during the interview
Lack of interest in the job offered
Poor appearance
Bad references
History of job hopping
Lack of education

Go ahead. Take a close look at that list again. Check off the reasons for failure that are easily avoidable. Incredible, isn't it?

The shoe also fits the other foot.

There is no doubt that in too many instances, the worker is seen as an expendable resource. "If this one doesn't work out or fails to show, not to worry. We'll get another."

Even where that attitude doesn't prevail, too often the employer does more than hire trouble, he asks for them.

Twenty percent of prospective employers fail to check references or education. Why? Often we just don't want to know. The schedule is short and you need a body. Maybe if you just don't ask, it won't be so. Yeh, right.

The biggest complaint we hear from our corporate clients is that quality applicants just don't apply. Got any ideas? Take a page out of Bill Clinton's book...it's the marketing.

Recruiting is a marketing problem. It is more important than anything else a manager can do. It is more important than anything else a manager can do. That's not a mistake; it's a point. Recruiting is a key management responsibility. More important than anything because it is a fact of business that customers go, not to the business with the lowest price, the best product or even the most convenient location. It is not price, product, packaging or place. It is the promise that the customer will feel good about the purchase decision.

And just what is it that contributes the most to the "promise of feel good?" Your employees. It is absolutely, positively impossible to build loyal customers without loyal, customer-focused employees.

FOUR DIMENSIONS

Recruiting, like all other marketing, is a matter of four dimensions: Desirability, believability, exclusivity and convenience.

Desirability

What have you done to make your place of business a desirable place to work? Just as you attempt to attract customers, you must do the same to attract quality employees. Who, in their right mind, would intentionally apply for a job where the working conditions were the pits? No one who had any other options.

If you are attracting the scum of the universe, know that your business is viewed as a resort for those with few other options. If you are scraping the bottom of the barrel, your job offer is right there with them.

What can you do today to make working for you a more attractive proposition?

And why would you want to spend even a dime to make working for you more attractive?

According to Leonard Schlesinger of the Harvard Business School as reported in the *Wall Street Journal*, companies that place a high value on recruiting, training and hiring, experience considerably, almost unbelievably better numbers than those who don't. Customer satisfaction and service quality jumps by more than 50 percent. The growth rate, compared to others in their industry is up by 60, to as much as 300 percent. And return on assets jumps an incredible 150 to 300 percent.

Do you believe those numbers? What if they were only half? What if we knocked them down to even 10 percent? It would still be worth it to immediately make recruiting, hiring and training your top priority. Why isn't it that way already?

Part of the problem is that work is so much like...well, work! A survey by *Industry Week* discovered that 70 percent of employees said their work was just plain not fun. And 63 percent described their workplace as "dog-eat-dog." (Take them off the lunch choice!)

I know there are some hard boiled eggs out there who are clenching teeth and thinking, "Well, damn it, work isn't supposed to be summer camp. It's supposed to be tough. It's tough for me. I'm here day and night making sure that the competition doesn't eat us alive. And it sure as hell wouldn't hurt you to at least work your eight-to-five without complaining."

Get a life!

The Sharper Image has a new gizmo called a Life Clock. It literally counts down the seconds left of your life based on your current age and the average life expectancy for your sex. I think they should also calculate a few less seconds to account for the psychological status of someone who would buy such a thing!

The truth is, work should be satisfying. It should make you feel like another day has ticked off the life clock and that even though you weren't exactly having a ball, you did spend those 266,400 seconds with people that you liked, doing things that were if not fun at least interesting.

What do employees think about their life on the job?

According to *Fortune* magazine, the Harris Company polled 3,707 people in fifteen countries and discovered that overall, work is a dreary form of torture (my interpretation...)

Percent who are...	U.S.	European Community	Japan
Very satisfied with work	43%	28%	17%
Proud of the product and service	65%	37%	35%
Say the pay is good	44%	26%	5%
Feel they can make a significant contribution	60%	33%	27%

Aren't we having fun? Look at the numbers and take a guess where customer service is nearly unheard of. Demming was right about one thing: Eighty percent of the problems with quality have little to do with the employee. They are the fault of the system.

And my corollary is that 100 percent of the problems with the system are caused by management.

Exclusivity

You know the old saw about supply and demand. Supply goes down and demand goes up. Why not treat your job openings like something special? Besides, if you don't, why would anyone else?

We recommend that you immediately stop interviewing and start auditioning.

An audition makes the job special. It moves you from "would you please take this job?" to a position of, "not everyone can qualify."

You don't have to be auditioning for astronauts for this to work. When the folks at Six Flags Over Texas began their hiring for the 1994 season, they extended the practice of auditioning all the way to the security department.

The same practice that was involved in landing a job as a singer or dancer in one of their many fine shows would now be employed in the search for folks to watch over security. Sixty positions attracted over four hundred eager applicants!

Believability

Like any good marketing proposition, the job offer can't be too good to be true. It has to be believable. Even for entry-level jobs, the offer has to be believable.

When my brother Gregg and I were in college, he called one afternoon to say that he would be late; he was interviewing for a job. He was excited because the ad that he responded to had painted a wonderful picture of high wages and a fun work environment with plenty of opportunity for advancement.

I held dinner, waiting to hear what promised to be good news. He finally came crawling through the door looking like he had been "rode hard and put up wet." There wasn't a trace of excitement. Instead he was mad enough to chew nails.

"How was it?"

"It was a miracle."

"Doesn't sound like a miracle."

"That's what they called it."

"Called what?"

"The miracle."

"I give up."

"They made a big deal out of the fact that we had been invited to participate in a modern day miracle. They said that we could play a part in revolutionizing the way people lived. Improve their health. Save them money. Give them back their leisure time. I had pictures of saving the world.

"Then they said, 'Gentlemen. You are about to witness a miracle.'

"Then they opened a side door and rolled in this machine. It had small wheels, an electric cord and a long flexible hose."

"'Sounds like a vacuum cleaner to me,' I laughed too soon.

"Looked like one, too. In fact, I said, 'That sure looks like a vacuum cleaner.' The guy said, 'Don't ever say that! This, gentlemen, is a miracle.' I just walked out. I thought I would save the miracles for someone who really needed one."

"So, why were you so late?"

"I stopped and got a job working for Sears. Not exactly a miracle, but heck, I like tools."

CONVENIENCE...AND COMFORT, TOO

Why do so many employers make working so darned inconvenient?

Why should work be convenient? It's what makes all that other frou-frou stuff possible. Work is our reason for being on the planet! You wish.

The truth is that the work ethics change or appear to change from generation to generation. Work should be, if not fun, at least tolerable. Yet, too many bosses take no pains at all to make working for them fit the rest of their employee's lifestyle. And today's worker is not nearly so dedicated to the job as is the boss.

The college students of today over and over cite freedom to do their own thing on their own time as the overwhelming force that drives their desire to start their own business. It's not the desire to get rich that was the motivation for generations past. Nope, today's worker wants more freedom and if we expect to attract and retain the best, we have to figure how to give them the freedom they seek while still getting the value out of the relationship.

Put another way, there has to be value for all parties in the work relationship. It is when we can determine how to get what we want by giving the other guys what they want that a win-win relationship is born.

There is another dimension that goes hand-in-hand with convenience, the dimension of comfort. When you look deeper into the reason for voluntary separation, the inevitable root cause seems to be stress. Stress? Yep, stress.

People don't leave jobs that they like, jobs where they are comfortable. We rarely figure the things about work that make work uncomfortable. Little things like training can make an incredible difference in turnover...all right, we'll be pc...retention rates. But don't train 'em and retention will seem like too mild of a word. They'll be turning over so fast that you'll be saying, "Training? We don't have time to train. No one ever stays long enough to be trained!"

When people are uncomfortable, they leave. I used to notice that new cooks at Denny's where I started growing up, seemed to go through phases that I later identified as Competent, Confident, Comfortable. Guys, and gals, too, would come in, hired as a cook-trainee and spend quite awhile learning the menu and tricks of the trade. (Try flipping eggs in a pan without breaking the yolks and you'll have a new appreciation for short-order cooks in short order.)

After they had pretty well mastered the skills, you would assume that they could be pretty much turned loose. Not even! It took a considerable amount of handholding well past the stage that they could, if left alone, handle things just fine. Trouble was, they couldn't stand to be left alone. Why? Because until you are competent, you won't develop confidence. And until you are confident, you definitely won't feel comfortable.

There are exceptions to the rule. We call them "cocky."

We get the big issues like air-conditioning and adequate lighting but we too often miss the little aggravations. Just as there are micro-insults that turn away our traditional customers, so are there little things that destroy relations with our internal customers.

Stuart, our videographer and resident techie, sat down to lunch today exclaiming, "You won't believe the new uniforms at..." and then he named a local quick-service restaurant. "They look like Pee Wee Herman's Big

Top in a collision with a Barnum and Bailey sideshow. I'd wear a dress before anybody could get me in those things."

Get it? There are a jillion things that we do to unnecessarily stress our employees and send them to work for our competitors. Some of them are little, dumb things like uniforms that make adults feel uncomfortable.

Joy Wright, president of Personnel/Performance Systems, Inc., of Bedford, Texas, gives us the top nine reasons for poor morale and the top reasons why employees leave. These lists are related, so here they are:

Poor Morale...

1. Poor working environment
2. Poor materials and equipment
3. Poor communications...not knowing what is expected, lack of recognition and feedback
4. Poor benefits
5. Poor pay
6. Lack of effective management and training
7. No employee orientation, sales training, product training, etc.
8. Poor parking facilities
9. No organized mission, vision or goals

Why employees leave...the other side of the coin

40%	Unhappy with management
20%	Management unhappy with them!
20%	Do not like the job
10%	Relocation
10%	Illness

Stop right here. Take a pencil and check off those things that you can control without spending a dime. Amazing, isn't it?

The United States now has a turnover rate of 4 percent per month. Compare that to 3.5 percent per year for Japan. You may have to read that again...that's a monthly turnover rate greater than an annual turnover rate. Figure the costs of recruiting, hiring and training. Figure the impact that turnover has on your customer service. Look at the costs of not getting it right...you can't afford to do this wrong!

SOMETHING MORE POSITIVE...

Exactly how do you go about hiring a team of winners? Follow these steps:

➢ Define what the customer thinks is a winner...develop a profile.

➤ Survey and improve your offer where possible.

➤ Audition to the profile.

➤ Create an individual training plan and get started.

➤ Survey to discover right up front what motivates your candidates individually.

➤ Create a performance contract to set standards of performance for both parties.

➤ Occasionally test your hiring decision against customer feedback.

➤ Occasionally test your training and incentive program against team-player feedback.

DEVELOPING THE PROFILE

You can ask your customers what kind of employee behavior makes them feel good about doing business with you and use that input to develop a hiring profile. Of course, there will be slightly different standards depending on the type of business, even depending on the particular job held within that business.

We had Joy Wright help us create a hiring profile to assist in hiring unit managers for a quick-service restaurant chain. What is important is that you don't decide up front the characteristics that you think would be handy and then ask for a profile that tests for them.

You begin by defining success in the job in question and then develop a profile to find similar successful people.

We took a huge sampling of unit managers and tested them against the standards of unit volume, sales growth and overall profitability. We were surprised to discover that the personality traits of successful unit managers were totally at odds with the traits of the successful assistant unit manager. Compared to the successful multi-unit managers, they looked like they were from outer space.

The lesson? There are no hard and fast rules for success when it comes to personality types.

Now, I'm going to contradict that statement. Sorta.

In a service economy there are a few personality traits that customers look for. These traits don't have to all be present in the same person or in the same mix. But, you had better have the majority of these traits present in at least some proportion or that customer just isn't going to love you.

What do they want? What should you want?

GREAT SERVICE WORKERS ARE...

> Gregarious...highly tolerant to customer contact
>
> Informed
>
> Articulate
>
> Inventive
>
> Able to work with minimum supervision
>
> Trustworthy
>
> Trainable

That's a short list of seven. Some of those traits you simply have to hire. Gregarious, informed, articulate, inventive, able to work with minimum supervision, trustworthy and trainable.

Okay, here's the evangelist in me coming out...you don't have to agree, but I do believe that every one of these traits can be taught to some degree. It may not be worth the incredible effort but it can be done. I see it being done every day.

It is done by example.

The problem is that few businesses have the luxury of having a non-performer in charge of their customers. And few businesses have the depth of management necessary and available to provide the hands-on coaching and in-your-face example that is needed to draw a quiet individual from their shell or coax a by-the-book employee into creative thinking or teach a slow starter to be a self-starter.

But I see it done every day. Some of my proudest moments have been when I heard a formerly shy, 16-year-old use my words but his initiative to play with a guest. Or when someone who could hardly decide where to park, take control of a busy rush, calling production and putting bodies in their places like a general on a battlefield.

Those small victories are luxuries. Most of the time we have to hire gregarious, articulate, trustworthy, trainable and inventive although we can usually train them to be informed and to work with minimum supervision.

WHILE WE'RE AT IT...

If the new economy is to be a wild-and-woolly service economy where only companies that are working lean and mean, thanks to highly entrepreneurial teams...well, better take a closer look at just what it means to be an entrepreneur.

Take my banker. Please.

In a favorite book, *Buy Low, Sell High, Collect Early and Pay Late*, author-professor Dick Levin describes his students going into banking as, "...good-looking, white, Protestant males of average intelligence with a low need to take risks and a high need for structured support systems..."

"And this," Levin continues, "is exactly what you, an entrepreneur, have to deal with when you walk in to get money. People who spend all of their lives taking risks — like you do — scare the hell out of most bankers." (Anecdotal evidence, I know, but darned if that doesn't describe my banker to a "T.")

Levin says that the only thing about bankers that is above average is their wardrobes. Obviously, he loves them!

Lowell Busenitz of Texas A&M University, College of Business Administration, surveyed over 200 executives divided almost evenly between corporate types and entrepreneurs. He wanted to discover if indeed there are differences between the two that would be significant and, if so, what those differences are. We have long heard that entrepreneurs don't operate on the same wavelength as the rest of the world but Busenitz set out in search of hard evidence.

In his survey, Busenitz discovered that entrepreneurs, as a class, rank high in the attributes of risk-taking and propensity to change. They scored lower than the corporate types in need for conformity, length of employment and education. I guess if you have plenty of education, you are too smart to jump off the cliff into the world of self-employment!

Entrepreneurs also beat the pants off their corporate counterparts in the attributes of outside reading and open thinking.

The big news that Busenitz uncovered is that entrepreneurs are much more likely to rely on intuition. Give them the facts but don't study it to death. Do something, anything.

Pinnacle Performance surveyed entrepreneurs to find out why they left corporate life.

Asked to list their top reasons for starting their own businesses, the responses were, in order of importance (partial list):

Felt I could make more money on my own.

Always wanted to own my own business.

Underutilization of my ability.

Needed autonomy/independence at work.

Incompetency of management.

Asked what they hoped would be different...

More opportunity to use all my skills and abilities.

More control of my life.

Being happy with my work.
Ability to create something.
Ability to grow professionally.
Autonomy or independence at work.
Fewer problems with internal politics.

Soooo What?

So, if independent, self-managed work teams are indeed the wave of the future, if skinny hierarchies will be the norm, if there are to be fewer supervisors...if we are to become the empowered organizations that we preach about, then we must hire and grow entrepreneurs!

We must help them achieve their personal goals in the context of large organizations. We must decide right now, that independent thinking is not a threat and do whatever it takes to hire independent people and harness their creativity.

Southwest Airlines understands the concept. They even put it to work.

We saw a recruiting ad for SWA that began with the headline, "Brian Shows An Early Aptitude For Working At Southwest Airlines." The facing page showed a coloring book outline of a dinosaur that had been colored with little regard to the lines. A Post-It note attached said, "Brian-Please try to color **inside** the lines!", followed by a teacher's smiling face.

SWA was implying that if you are interested in thinking on your own, in coloring dinosaurs any way they look good to you, then maybe SWA is the perfect work environment.

When was the last time you actively went in search of people who knew how to color outside the lines? When have you put more emphasis on intuition than wardrobe? When have you spent time thinking about how to encourage free-thinking and discourage the reactive, "Yes, Boss?"

2

WHILE WE'RE LOOKING...

You could say that there are only three basic attributes to consider when hiring...can do, will do and fit. The idea of fit is an especially important consideration as we begin to restructure work around self-managed teams.

Not every sharp, positive individual is a perfect hire. That's because they must also fit the team in several ways.

First, they must have a personality that can be accepted by the team. This isn't exactly marriage but it's close. A loner, a non-team player just isn't going to be productive working on a team no matter what the skills. Some folks just aren't team players. They don't deserve to be shunned but neither do they deserve to be set up for failure by being asked to work in an environment where they will be the social outcast. They may be perfect for more entrepreneurial endeavors.

Second, new hires should have skills and personalities that complement those of the rest of the team. If you graphed the personality traits of successful sales staff, you would be surprised to discover that they are almost exactly 180 degrees out of sync with those of successful service staff.

That is not to say that great sales people have nothing in common with great servers or that they are not capable of giving terrific service. It is only to make the point that they are different and that it is important to recognize the fact that we all come with a slightly different set of skills and talents.

Great leaders take individuals with differences and harness those differences for the good of the team.

On our team, even though we truly do love each other, we are all as different as night is to day. Stuart loves to edit...Donna loves to shoot...Betty (Mom) is great on the phone but don't ask her to speak...which Cindy loves...while Joe thinks that selling is the most fun you can have as long as you don't ask him to stay in the office...where Jim and Kristine are most comfortable because they don't like the idea of travel...which is the stuff of Melanie's daydreams...and not at all of interest to Julie who really prefers to slip into the office and do her work in the wee hours of the morning so she can be gone before I come in just after dawn! The perfect team. We coordinate but do not match!

What does a perfect team player look like? Depends on the team. And the team profile depends on the task and the customer.

Whatever you do, don't be hesitant to keep the crew on the skinny side. Teams that are pushed, (but not whipped), perform better than teams that have been allowed to grow until they are fat and lazy.

Mark Sanborn, author-speaker-consultant, who specializes in working with teams and, author of *TeamBuilt*, says that inappropriately-sized teams each produce unwanted symptoms. Teams can be too big as well as too small.

These aren't exactly Mark's lists, but you'll get the idea...

Team too small...
Difficulty producing desired results
Missed deadlines
Long, sometimes abusive hours
Team members involved in trivial decisions
Outside help needed too often

Team too large...
Lack of camaraderie
Don't understand what others do
Low levels of interaction
Members feel uninformed
Problems happen without everyone being aware
Members become territorial

IMPROVE THE OFFER...

When you have determined the profile that you want to hire against, it's time to review the offer. Remember, you don't have to have an outstanding offer but it must stand out. It must be just a little bit better than what is standard for the industry. Or, it will have to be a little bit better than what it would take to attract comparable talent from related industries.

Pay is only one part of the offer. There are dozens of no or low-cost perks that can greatly enhance your offer if you are flexible enough to live with them. Flexibility is, itself, probably the greatest addition to your hiring offer that you could make and it rarely costs a dime.

The Roper Organization surveyed to find out what is most important to Americans. They came up with this list in order of importance:

1. The education of their children
2. Family health
3. Their own health
4. Quality of life
5. Friends and relatives
6. Love life
7. Income and standard of living
8. Their occupation
9. Leisure activities
10. The current political situation

Did you find the name of your company anywhere on that list? If it is mentioned even obliquely, it is all the way near the bottom. Number eight to be exact. Does that tell you anything about your job offer?

We survey our people to find out what they really want out of their work experience. I keep a copy on a computer file that I often review just before any long meetings with anyone on our team. It's nice to know the little personal, emotional goodies that make them tick, to be able to meet their needs often with only a word or some simple permission.

Flexible hours, special training, even membership in a prized professional organization can be powerful incentives to sign on. Now that you know that, why not begin thinking about improving your offer to the folks you have already hired? Begin by conducting, and this can be very informal, a short audit of your offer. Do you offer childcare, eldercare, flexible hours, ownership, a comfortable work environment?

AUDITION TO THE PROFILE...

Even though we've already mentioned auditioning, there is an additional dimension that you should consider. That is the idea of assessment, the practice of putting executives in situations similar to those that they may encounter while on the job.

The idea has been around for decades and even though it is extremely effective, it remains way underutilized. The idea is simple. Before you make the final offer, take the candidate into a real work experience, stand back and watch.

For example, if you are "auditioning" for salespersons, take the leading candidates on a sales call or two. You can sacrifice a low probability sales call or ask a favorite customer to participate. Customers love to be involved in your hiring process.

Southwest Airlines actually has employed a panel of frequent flyers to assist in hiring flight attendants. And why not? If you are hiring people with the express priority of pleasing customers, it stands to reason that customers are best prepared to make the final go/no–go decision.

The purpose of the audition is to verify your first impressions of the applicant. First impressions are almost always right and even when they are not, they are all that really counts in a service economy, which is, when you think about it, rarely more than a matter of first impression.

If the first impression is not a good one, pass. Period. You can't tell a customer in a service industry that "Old Harry is a little rough. Stick around. After a while, he'll grow on you." Well, mold will grow on you. In a service business, every business, the first impression is about all that you get.

The audition is only to verify that what you have seen so far is what you will be likely to get after the hire and when there are a zillion customers screaming for fast, friendly service.

Believe it or not, labor is always a seller's market. That's because employees are quite capable of giving you considerably more than the performance required to keep their job. In fact, only a paltry two of ten employees give 100 percent on the job. The other 80 percent are working somewhere between their very best and what little it takes to keep from being canned.

Down-sizing has made us all work skinny. There isn't going to be room for folks who don't or won't pull their weight. It's not a bad idea to be right up front and let candidates know that, "If you don't like to sweat...this job's not for you." You can even do a little "unselling" up front to save you grief down the road.

In an audition, you are looking for signs that when it comes to the emotional labor that is service work, the employee is motivated by the desire to serve others, that the employee is turned on by doing for others.

When you see a natural-born, customer-service type, you will want to sell them on the prospect of working for you. Don't do that. It destroys that idea of exclusivity.

Instead, take a coy position while still communicating the idea that your job, this job, is highly desirable. If you need to sell, do it like this... "The selected candidate will be...."

Get it? Don't sell.

If you really want to put science on your side, consider a personality test. Be absolutely certain that you are working with a pro. A test that hasn't been validated for the job is worse than no test at all; it's a lawsuit looking for funding.

Even without a formal test, you can get a pretty good feel for the individual's ability to tolerate high customer contact. (High customer contact is a term originally coined by Ron Zemke to describe the ability to handle one customer after another without going absolutely crazy.)

My suggestion for high customer contact jobs? Hire folks who are already crazy!

When you have your profile in hand or at least in mind...stick to it. We are all inclined to go for the easy hire and that is often a matter of promoting from within. Okay, we agree that promoting from within can be great for employee morale, short term. But, please, admit that it can be disastrous for both morale and profitability in the long run.

Promoting from within is often a matter of hiring the best of the worst.

As an example, if you have eight unit managers, none of whom are particularly impressive, which would you pick when their supervisor leaves for whatever reason? Promote from within? It's great for morale but remember that none of your choices were what you would describe as outstanding at managing their unit. Is this the person you want to leave in charge of the entire group?

It seems the best you could hope for is all the units would eventually come up to the more or less sorry standards of the newly promoted supervisor's old operation.

Carry this scenario to its illogical extreme. A few months later, you have an opening one level up. You look around at your multi-unit supervisors and discover all had been in-house promotions of not particularly stellar performers. Keep it up and you can breed so much mediocrity throughout the organization that it will become the norm, no longer even recognizable as mediocre.

"But, if I don't promote from within, the troops will be demoralized!"

Not if you have a definite standard that is known and followed.

One of our customers sent us a sheet torn from his desktop calendar that reads... "The one thing I know: The only ones among you who will be really happy are those who have sought and found how to serve."

Then it gives a multiple choice response listing Clara Barton, St. Paul and Albert Schweitzer. (I'll guess Schweitzer.)

Hah! I was right! Albert Schweitzer (1875-1965).

3

TRAINING PLAN

Adults learn and like to learn differently than children. Careful! All adults are not adult learners. We're really talking a matter of maturity here. So don't assume that just because the person standing in front of you is tall enough to ride the "E" attractions that you are indeed dealing with an adult.

Adult learning...

➢ Should be information that applies directly to the task.
➢ Should always include the "why" as well as the "how" of the process.
➢ Should be learning that the adult can control both pace and order. (Adults like to be in control.)
➢ Should take into account the learner's experience. (Adults hate being taught material that they have already mastered.)
➢ Should involve the learners and allow them to share their experiences.

This means that adult learning should be learner-controlled and customized for each learner. This isn't as difficult as you think. It just takes a little adjusting. For example, you can break learning into modules and allow trainees to choose which order they take them. There should always be a "test out" option. If the learner can pass the test...course over, next!

Whatever you do, do not lower standards. No one likes to face the customer or the task not feeling fully prepared.

SURVEY TO DISCOVER MOTIVATORS

We've covered this ground but haven't mentioned when to survey.

New employees should be surveyed right up front and surveyed again shortly after assuming their new job position. Survey again within sixty or ninety days and every six months or so thereafter.

CREATE PERFORMANCE CONTRACTS

The price of membership to a team should be the willingness to contribute to its success. If that is so, it is important to post that price clearly, right up front, so there can be no doubt about it. Team players should know exactly what is expected before they are invited to play.

Every employee should be on an individual performance contract that explicitly defines what constitutes good performance. And, as with any good contract, the employee should be told right up front exactly what to expect in terms of support, training and compensation.

What? You don't want to put that in writing? Well, I don't want to work for you!

Performance contracts should include...

➢ Pay and benefits
➢ How and when training is to occur
➢ Expected performance during the training process
➢ On-the-job performance broken into training, familiarization and final phases

Here's a sample performance contract...

Joe Jefferson is hired to sell video services for VidTec, Inc., on a commission plus expenses basis. There will be a draw against commission paid at the rate of $____/ month.

Commissions will be paid according to the attached commission schedule.

Joe is expected to sell a minimum of $____ in video production within the first forty-five days from the date of hire. He is expected to sell at least $____ in video production during the next sixty days after which he will be paid on straight commission and authorized expenses only.

VidTec agrees to send Joe to the next industry-sponsored sales certification training course, provide a complete orientation as agreed by Joe and send the sales manager on a minimum of twenty sales calls which will be determined by Joe.

This agreement specifically does not guarantee continued employment. The employee can and will be terminated for failure to perform as stated, failure to follow company policy and may be terminated for any other reason without notice.

The above agreement tells exactly how and when the employee will be paid, what is the expected performance and how the employee will be supported in terms of training. Also outlined are the employee's responsibilities.

TEST HIRING DECISIONS AGAINST CUSTOMER FEEDBACK

Employees should never feel invincible although they should be made to feel safe. Employees who feel as though they cannot be terminated are a disaster to customer service. (Look at government employees and government service. Look at the Post Office. Look at most unionized operations where terminating an employee requires an act of God or, in some cases, Congress. Customer service goes right out the window whenever employees feel invincible.)

When supervisors are forced to arbitrate employee grievances with union stewards, the very idea goes out the window in favor of Them vs. Us conflict.

For the rest of the world, frequently test your hiring decisions against customer feedback. Notice please that we didn't say that a single, irate, unreasonable customer should have life and death say-so over any employee. What we are saying is that customers, plural, should have a definite impact on compensation and placement decisions.

More later.

TEST TRAINING AND INCENTIVE PROGRAMS AGAINST INTERNAL CUSTOMER FEEDBACK

Just because you have a program in place should not guarantee its continued existence. Employees change, situations change. So training and incentive programs cannot be installed and expected, like a cosmic perpetual motion machine, to stay in place forever. On a regular basis, ask, survey, find out how these programs are working.

The purpose of incentive programs is not only to exact greater performance; they should also be created with the idea in mind of making it difficult to leave. Keep your offer just a little more attractive than the competition and turnover won't be a problem. Find out what floats their boat and then float it!

CONTINGENT WORKER

There is one major trend that may in some ways be the master people trend, the rise of the professional contingent worker. As organizations begin to flatten, work formerly done by in-house professional support staff will become the purview of the professional contingent worker. With them, they bring years of experience, probably learned compliments of a major corporation that helped them make the decision to strike out on their own.

They also bring a new set of problems.

How do you incorporate these permanent outsiders into the mission and vision of the organization? How do you get and keep their loyalty and confidentiality?

Here's what to do...

➤ Use permanent outsiders.
➤ Include the new contingent professional in your orientation program.
➤ Sell them on the vision right up front...treat them as partners.
➤ Acquaint them with the corporate team right away even include them in incentive programs and feedback systems.

UN-HIRING

Don't you just love it when big corporations begin to imitate the idiocy of government and create euphemisms for the dumbest things? Taxes become revenue enhancements. Criminals become perpetrators or even victims. Combat becomes police action and mass layoffs become right-sizings.

So why not learn to un-hire?

The first rule in un-hiring is to un-hire before the employee quits because employees usually quit before they leave.

When an employee has decided, for whatever reason, to stop working at their best, they need to be immediately un-hired. When you have done everything that you know to do to create a positive, motivating work environment and have failed to find the spark that ignites performance, it is time to consider un-hiring.

Contrary to what union organizers will tell the public, I don't know a single employer, large or small, who fails to feel personally the pain of terminating employees for whatever reason. I have cried many times. I know others who have done just the same when faced with the awful task of cutting someone loose.

But with the joy of leadership comes the burdens, chief of which is the responsibility to make the tough decisions. Decisions that, although may be devastating to the individuals involved, are necessary for the well-being of the team that remains.

If there is one fault that I find with business leaders, in general, it is that they are too slow to coach and counsel. When they wake up to the morning-after-headache of poor hiring compounded by worse management, they wait far too long to the face the reality that someone has got to go.

The moment that it becomes absolutely clear that one of your players has become an unsalvageable liability to the team, un-hire.

SELECTION...

If there is a single most critical task of leadership, it has to be the responsibility to assemble the finest team possible. Great teams can survive poor tactical leadership. Great teams make great leaders because great leaders make great teams. There are no great leaders without great teams.

4

SHAPING PERFORMANCE

Hi! I'll be your server tonight and I sure hope that you'll be patient. This is my first day on the job and you are my very first customers!"

"Perfect! This is our first time here so we can figure this out together!"

We gave her our order taking extra care to help her get it just right. I told her that we had all been in the restaurant business and felt quite at home in coffee shops so she should relax since we had all experienced first-day jitters.

When the order came, she saved mine for last. She placed it on the table, turning her head as she did, saying, "I don't think you are going to want this."

She was right. It was the burned carcass of what had once been a patty melt. Not just overdone, mind you, we're talkin' still smokin' b-u-r-n-e-d burned.

"Let me give you a little training. You don't have to pick up any order that you wouldn't eat. There's no reason for you to have to feel guilty about anything that you serve."

"Should I ask the cook to make you another one?"

"Not in this case. This isn't a simple oops. There's no way the cook couldn't know that this is totaled. No, let's ask the manager to step over here."

"I can't believe that was served. First my apologies. Second, please order anything that you wish and it will be on the house. Is there anything else I can do to make this right?"

"As a matter of fact, there is. I'd like you to take this sandwich to your office."

"To my office?"

"And take the cook with you. And don't let either one of them out until..."

"One of them has eaten the other?"

"You got it!"

Why would I have made that suggestion? All in the name of science and feedback?

We often see really mondo-bizarro behavior and can't for the life of us figure why people would do such strange things. Well, here is the answer. With a few exceptions, people aren't stupid even when they do stupid things. They are, rather, ignorant. This describes a large percentage of our population. That's the bad news.

The good news is that even if they have selected you as their boss, ignorant can be fixed. With a little patience and a chapter of basic information, you can become a fixer of ignorance par excellence.

Read on! We'll show you why people do stupid things especially at work. And then we'll show you how to make things better, how to help your team players discover their own magnificence. (They really are magnificent, you know, and we're going to help you help them find it!)

Let's look back at the waitress, the manager and the cook. Each played a part that, believe it or not, was almost impossible to have been played otherwise. The waitress (I know that's not exactly politically correct) was bright and pleasant. She did something, if you think about it, was really rather dumb. She brought a smoking sandwich to a customer knowing full well that not even a fire-eater could have digested it.

The cook's behavior was inexcusable...but very explainable.

And the manager? Obviously trained.

Just what does it mean to be trained?

The answer may be as simple as ABC...antecedents, behaviors and consequences.

Don't worry. Even though this sounds like we are about to dive into a deep academic discussion, we're not. And I promise, that if you like working with people, you'll probably find the rest of this chapter very interesting because it will help you understand why people do what they do and give you a few simple tools for getting them to do what you want them to do.

Behavior never stands alone. There is always a trigger and a consequence. Something causes it. Something happens as a result. The results of one behavior usually become antecedents for more behavior.

The phone rings and...right, you answer. That's the antecedent and the behavior. It's also the natural order of things. (Worry if you start answering the phone before it rings. That's behavior I can't help you explain.)

Imagine that you are sitting comfortably in your favorite chair with a snack balanced precariously on your lap and a book in your hand. The phone rings.

"Darn!"

You get out of the chair, race to the phone so you can pick up the phone before the answering machine kicks in. You say a pleasant, "Hello?" and some jerk who has dialed a wrong number just hangs up. Antecedent, behavior and consequence.

Back into your chair, page recovered and a fresh bite of snack when...the phone rings. (Antecedent) Once again you race to catch it before the machine gets it. You muster another cheerful,"Hello?" (Behavior) only to be rewarded by silence followed by a "click." (Consequence)

On the way to the chair you think evil thoughts, conjure up Draconian laws and, in general, wish an early death for any idiot who would be so ill-bred as to not at least say, "Sorry," before hanging up and retreating to his cave.

Back into your chair, the phone rings again. (Antecedent) You race from your chair, pick up the phone, only this time there is no breath wasted on a cheery, "Hello?"

This time you let the Neanderthal have it both barrels, mincing no words, even inventing a few in the process. (Behavior)

It's your Mom. (Consequence and Antecedent for the next time the phone rings no matter what the circumstance!)

And that's how behavior works. Antecedents trigger Behaviors that yield Consequences that become the Antecedent for the next behavior. Simple but not the entire story.

AUNTIE C DENT...

What would you guess are antecedents found in the typical work environment? How about tools, training aids, directional signs, the telephone (of course), certain co-workers, anything that causes you or reminds you to perform a task.

Speaking one day to Holiday Inns Worldwide, I was on my third back-to-back, fifty-minute presentation. For short presentations, I generally use more humor and less audience interaction. About fifteen minutes into the presentation something awful happened.

I couldn't decide if the story that I had in mind was one I had just told or if it was in my mind because I was getting ready to tell it. I skipped the story and left out one of my best pieces of material.

After the presentation, I still hadn't decided if the material had been omitted but as I reached to put on my suit coat, I realized what had been the problem. For this particular story, I remove my coat and do a funny impression. I realized that I had failed to put my coat back on after the second presentation so that when I got to the story in the third presentation, I was not wearing my coat.

Removing the coat had become a cue, an antecedent of sorts, to the telling of the story. No antecedent, no story.

Antecedents work best when they are specific and when they accurately predict consequences. A ringing telephone is a very specific antecedent. (In this country, telephones are extremely reliable. They ring and chances are, you've got a call.)

Behaviors that immediately precede another behavior can be antecedents such as the behavior of removing my coat served as an antecedent for telling the story. There can be whole strings of behaviors that become antecedent to the next. And in my case, a little laughter or applause or even the occasional "ah hah," is the consequence I need to stay motivated.

Speaking to Federal Express, a super group of folks, I looked into the audience and noticed my client giving me a rather unusual hand signal. I had no idea what it meant. I went deeper into my story. The signal got wilder. I thought she was really getting into it. I really poured it on. (There's nothing like an appreciative audience. Her hand signals could have directed a huge brass band. I thought I must be doing something totally awesome.)

After the presentation, she came rushing to me, thrilled I was certain.

"Why in the world didn't you stop when I signaled to you?"

"You were signaling stop? Stop? As in don't do that?"

"Yes! Stop as in 'I thought you were about to tell a different story that would have gotten you killed in this crowd!'"

"Sorry."

I have no idea what was the story that I didn't tell but it's a good thing I hadn't been running down that track because those signals (antecedents) weren't enough to stop me.

To be effective, antecedents must be very specific **and** predict consequences.

Think about that annoying couple who never visit without dragging along what has to be the world's most vicious two-year-old. The kid has a penchant for kicking anyone who doesn't kick back.

"Now, Johnny, don't be mean to the nice man. Mommy might have to get angry with you."

Now, what kind of dumbhead antecedent is that? "...don't be mean...Mommy might get angry..." Nah, nah, nah. Give me a break.

My mom would have nailed the concept and the kid.

"Sit down this instant! Kick him one more time and I'll blister your backside!"

Now that's an antecedent!

Want to make antecedents that have real power? Then make certain that they communicate exactly what kind of behavior is expected and be certain that you connect them solidly to the consequences.

Do what? "Sit down..."

When? "This instant!"

Or what? "I'll blister your backside!"

Mom...master of antecedents.

None of this "Let's take a little time out, dear." Like a two-year-old can understand the threat that you won't let him get his driver's license the instant he turns sixteen. Two-year-olds can understand a quick swat on their padded butts. (Notice, please, that I am not advocating beating children or e-v-e-r acting in anger.)

Some antecedents are just more effective than others. Swat the kiddo and then get on with living. No point in making a huge, dragged out analogy for a two-year-old who won't get it anyway. Let the kiddo make his own rules.

"Gee, everytime I jump on the couch, that guy swats me. I know, I'll make a new rule...never jump on the couch...when the big guy is around!"

When employees are not behaving, call that performing, up to standard, look first at the antecedents.

> Have you clearly detailed the expected behavior?

> Can there be any doubt or misinterpretation?

> Are the performers aware of the consequences, both positive and negative, of their behavior?

> Is there a history of certain consequence?

RELIABLE REWARD, REINFORCEMENT AND RECOGNITION

When we talk about reward, reinforcement and recognition, we're really only talking about three variations on a central theme...feedback. In its simplest form, feedback is nothing more than what workers everywhere ask or dream of asking, "Tell me how I'm doing."

Everyone wants feedback. Former New York Mayor Ed Koch made feedback famous as he walked the streets asking constituents, "How'm I doin'?"

Feedback is a form of consequence. Contrary to the popular understanding, not all feedback is verbal nor is it always negative.

The most effective feedback is...

Immediate
Positive
Specific
Personalized
Self–monitored
Related to baseline performance
Easily understood
Sincere

Feedback is always immediate...to something. Where leaders make their feedback mistakes is in delaying praise or criticism. No matter what you say, the performer always associates the feedback with whatever behavior immediately preceded it. That's why the old, "Wait till your father comes home," just doesn't work.

First of all, by the time Dad comes rolling into the driveway, the kiddo has completely forgotten the transgression that is about to be transferred to his backside. The association will be Dad = punishment, a great way to bring the family together. (The second reason that this is counterproductive behavior is that in 50 percent or more homes, there is no father. "Hey, Mom! Why don't we just hold off on the punishment gig until the old man comes around!")

We overheard this conversation:

"You won't believe what Joan did. She left the station a total mess."

"What did you do about it?"

"I put a 'hot' letter in her file. I'll let her have it when her evaluation rolls around next April."

"That ought to fix her."

Yeh, right. Can you imagine when April rolls around and the supervisor whips out that letter telling about a transgression leftover from the previous summer? What is the only logical conclusion that the employee will be able to draw?

"She must be out to get me. If this was really important, she would have talked to me about it at the time. She must have just written that letter. I wonder what I did this week that got her so upset?"

Immediate and positive. If you want to encourage behavior, keep the feedback positive. Positive feedback gets more of a behavior. Negative feedback does not get more of the desired behavior; it only works to stop undesired behaviors. But a leader's job is not to go around stopping poor performance. A leader's job is to encourage great performance.

Great leaders are masters of well-timed, highly focused positive feedback.

Unfortunately, we don't always know what constitutes positive feedback. Really. And worse, even when we do give positive feedback, we're only effective about 20 percent of the time. Surveys show that supervisors believe they give positive feedback more than five times as often as team players think that they get positive feedback.

Specific feedback carries more clout.

"I really like the way you handled that last customer. The way you were able to pick up on the clue that she was unhappy with our delivery."

Get it? The more specific, the more positive the more impact.

Compare the above with..."You have a nice way with customers..." So much mush that the performer may not even take the comment seriously and look instead for an ulterior motive.

Personalized feedback has impact for obvious reasons. Everyone likes to hear their name mentioned in a positive light. But personalized feedback is better for a less obvious reason...there is no hiding the fact that it is intended to relate to my behavior. Not that of the team. Not that of the entire organization. Me. My behavior is noticed and it obviously must count.

One of the most overlooked methods of increasing the value of feedback is the idea of involving the performer. Feedback systems that include charts, graphs and other forms of reporting have much greater impact when the performer involved is left to collect the data and post the results.

One of the most effective shapers of performance that we use in our office is called the "Monday Measures." Every Monday, everyone is expected to post the previous week's progress on the electronic bulletin board. Each individual posts his or her accomplishments as well as the plan for the coming week.

We post sales, dollars delivered, wins (work that made a difference but that is not easily measured in dollars) and we complete an entry titled, On the List. We also list what we are reading. Trust me no one wants to post a zip Monday Measure.

Look at how our Monday Measures would be received differently if it were compiled and posted by the office staff. Would it have as much impact? Could it ever be perceived as negative or punitive?

Most important, as we create feedback systems, we need to keep in mind that human beings need targets or benchmarks against which to evaluate or judge their performance. Feedback systems work best when they represent performance compared to some baseline or standard.

Examples:

➤ Sales compared to sales the same period last year.
➤ Production compared to same period last month.
➤ Defects per thousand compared to the same measurement for the previous period.

Feedback gives targeting data. In the military, the artillery rely on spotters, individuals who call in the coordinates of a target and report on how close the first round was to the target so the gunners can make adjustments. Feedback is nothing more than targeting data provided with the intention of helping the performer make corrections. That's why smart managers don't wait for perfect performance before providing positive feedback.

Poor feedback is found at the root of almost every instance of poor performance.

The psychologists call the idea of reinforcing improving behavior "reinforcement of successive approximations of the desired performance." All that means is that the performance must continue to improve in order for the positive feedback to continue.

Feedback can be both consequence and reinforcement, especially because no one wants to perform poorly. No one wants to perform poorly. (Not an editing mistake, just a darned important point.) Feedback that is properly delivered is almost always welcome because it helps the performer improve.

SEND IN THE REINFORCEMENTS

Reinforcement is a positive consequence that follows a behavior (performance) and increases the likelihood that the behavior will be repeated.

Reinforcement doesn't have to be material but verbal reinforcement is often more effective if accompanied by something tangible.

What can you do to improve the effectiveness of the reinforcement that you give?

Let's answer the question by expanding our view of reinforcement. There is reinforcement, reward and a special version of the two, recognition.

Where management often fails is not in providing reinforcement that has maximum value to the performer. Do you remember when you were a kid and the big prize for selling the most band candy was a cheap two-transistor radio? (If you don't, don't tell me. I've already flown past forty.)

Back then that was a heck of a prize...oooohhhhh! A radio!! But what kid today would walk across the street for a two-transistor radio if you were giving them away?

The point is simple...it doesn't matter what you think is a good reinforcement. Reinforcement is only in the eyes of the beholder.

What can you use for reinforcement? Use a WHIP, of course! No, not whip, but WHIP — Whatever you Have In your Pocket. We've seen small pieces of candy, tickets to the ball game, an invitation to lunch and even the boss's tie used very effectively as reinforcement. Effective reinforcement does not have to be costly, only desired by the performer.

The best way to find out what are the most effective reinforcers is, of course, to ask.

Many companies recognize that one man's trash is another's treasure and use outside fulfillment houses to help them create incentive programs that allow participants to choose from a catalogue of goodies to find their reinforcement. Winners are given dollar or point values and use their allotment to shop for exactly what floats their boat.

Point: The catalogues are usually distributed when the program is introduced so that a particular goodie can capture the imagination right up front and act as an antecedent to winning behavior.

Even when a lot of dollars are spent on reinforcement, reinforcement used effectively has a greater return on investment than new equipment, training, anything!

For more effective **delivery** of reinforcement...

➤ Make certain that the reinforcement is perceived as such.
➤ Make it personal.
➤ Reinforce immediately.
➤ Reinforce frequently.
➤ Make the reinforcement behavior specific.
➤ Never use the "sandwich" method.
➤ Never reinforce and punish at the same time.

PART VI

THE NEW LEADER

1

NEW COMMANDMENTS

Of the best leader, when he is gone,
They will say: We did it ourselves.

Chinese proverb

The new leader is beginning to emerge. He is often a she. He...or she, is passionate, committed and focused. The new leader looks like the old leader except that it's just possible there are more of them. And it's just possible that we're finally coming to value the difference between leadership and management.

One word uniquely defines the new leader, "values." For the past several years, we've been struggling to articulate the new leadership values in the form of ten commandments. First we took our solo shot, then we listened and listened again. We think we finally have it but wouldn't be surprised if we had to adjust again. (If you'd like a laminated copy of the Ten Commandments for Leaders, call 800-635-7524, M-F, 9 a.m. to 4 p.m. CST.)

> ## TEN COMMANDMENTS FOR LEADERS
>
> Be a quality fanatic.
> Be a service champion.
> Value action.
> Build teams and leaders.

197

> Make integrity an issue.
> Make work fun.
> Anticipate tomorrow.
> Break the rules, honor the values.
> Manage first, labor second.
> Lead from the heart.

BE A QUALITY FANATIC

We once had a client famous for saying that "good enough rarely is." Although we experienced that they neither believed nor practiced that admonition, it has made a dramatic difference in the way we do business.

At our restaurant, I could no longer pass a scrap of paper or cigarette butt without stopping to pick it up. Where I once could have picked up the big pieces and said, "That's good enough for now," I now had to pick up every piece and sweep, too.

(I believe if the crew saw me coming and wanted an extra few minutes to get things in shape that they would have tossed out an odd scrap or two just to slow me down!)

When you talk to the leaders of today who are making a difference, the one commonality is their absolute fanaticism for doing things as close to perfect as possible. One example that caught my eye was the headline of an ad for General Motors that read, "We blew a deadline, ticked everyone off, cost the company a bundle and we did the right thing."

The ad continues to tell about a Chevrolet division manager who, well, let's let the copy writers tell it...

"What if you ran a divison of General Motors and were due to debut an important flagship model...and it wasn't quite ready yet? Nothing drastic, you understand, just a few glitches that meant that not every car coming off the line was just right. What if you'd sworn to your bosses that you'd be ready? What if you had a lot of potential customers waiting to get a first look? What would you do? Here's what Jim Perkins and his team did: they pulled the plug on the introduction and said, 'When we know we've got it right, we'll bring out the car.' That night, Jim Perkins did what people who do the right thing always do. He got a good night's sleep."

Be a quality fanatic. Not concerned about quality. Not interested in quality. Not even aggressive about quality although that's getting close. Be a quality f-a-n-a-t-i-c!

The corollary to this commandment that is specifically targeted to leaders is this:

Be a visible standard of excellence.

An old trainer's trick shows up in my presentation notes as "hand-to-chin." It's a silly version of Simon Says. I have the audience stand and follow my actions as I shout, "Put your hands up...now out...now back up...now straight forward, that's good...now put them back up...now, grab your chin! Grab your chin! Grab your chin!"

Of course, I'm holding my cheek, and so is everyone else.

The point? People learn by doing. The things that they will do are things that they see in their environment and can imitate. No matter how sophisticated your training program and materials, no matter what catchy slogans you may have adopted, in the end, the things that people actually do are those things that they see being done and can imitate.

That makes you, the leader, THE training program.

People learn each and every time they interact with their environment. If they act and get a rewarding reaction, the behavior will be repeated. If the boss is leading the way, walking the talk as well as talking the talk, the likelihood that the team member will try out the behavior increases exponentially.

Leaders have one overriding responsibility, to act as a visible standard of excellence.

There is good news and bad news here.

The standard, like it or not, is always visible. Unfortunately, it is not always a standard of excellence.

Our friend, Al DeLiberto walked into the kitchen of his restaurant, Boccone's, and noticed immediately that something didn't smell just the way it was supposed to smell. Instead of the lure of fresh-baked bread, Al, who has a nose like a bloodhound (we're talking ability not size), noticed that something smelled, well, sorta burnt.

"What's going on with the bread?"

"We sorta overcooked it."

"Why is it on the rack and not in the trash?"

"There's a lot of it."

"So?"

"It's almost time for dinner."

"So, toss it! We can afford to dump the bread. We can't afford to lose our customers."

Quality f-a-n-a-t-i-c.

What cost-driven managers appear to misunderstand is the fact that every ad, every slogan, every word in a commercial or on the package is a promise. Customers used to be a lot more forgiving when the product failed to meet the promise. That has all changed.

No longer is caveat emptor the law of the land. Buyer beware has become one shot and you're dead. There are too many quality operators chasing your customers to risk not keeping the promise. Our marketing creates a level of expectation that simply must be met. Promise little and deliver the same and the customers are relatively satisfied. Fail to deliver the promise and you will find yourself on thin ice.

We are constantly reminded to underpromise and overdeliver. There is a reason. The difference between Positively Outrageous Service and outrageously bad service is nothing more than a matter of expectations. POS is defined as service that is random and unexpected, out-of-proportion to the circumstance and personally involves the customer, resulting in compelling word-of-mouth.

What do you suppose is the definition of the worst service you ever had? Back up a sentence or two and find out.

The definition of the worst service and the definition of the best service is exactly the same. It all revolves around the expectation. Go to McDonald's and get Mickey D quality and you think you have a value. Get the same food at Chez Whatever at twenty-five bucks a head and you feel robbed. The difference? A matter of expectation.

Top leaders are masters of managing expectations. They also do whatever it takes to make only those promises that they can keep and are fanatical about keeping them.

We've been asked a hundred times about the restaurant mentioned in our first book, *Positively Outrageous Service*. We sold it. Why? It was clean. The food was good. The service was fine. But, it had stopped being what I call Positively Outrageous Service. And POS was our promise. So, rather than attempt to run a restaurant by remote control while I traveled the country to preach POS, we stopped making that promise.

What promises are you making right now? What are you promising your customers? Your team players? Yourself?

Be A Service Champion

What does it mean to be a service champion? It means to be on constant watch for ways to say "yes" to the customer. Service champions wouldn't dream of trying to fit customers into the system. Instead, they make the system fit the customer.

"When would you like it delivered?"

"What color works best for you?"

"How would you like to pay for this?"

Service champions would rarely say, "We can't do that." Or, "That's not my job."

Service champions take responsibility for pleasing the customer. They have a "Whatever it takes," philosophy to service. I guess that's why it's so important in a service business, and that's every business, to hire only folks who get their kicks out of serving others.

Service champions listen. If you can't fill the order until you hear it, listening to the customer has to be the number one service skill. Service champions listen and then act.

VALUE ACTION

The new leader has a bias for action. Sometimes that's interpreted to mean that half-baked ideas are good ideas. They are not. But having a bias for action means that when the idea has been tested thoroughly, you don't keep on testing. Too many managers, probably out of fear, which says something about their leaders, research and test an idea half to death before they finally let it go.

If this commandment seems at odds with the first commandment, read again.

Fear motivates too many decisions. If you find yourself being motivated by fear, my advice? Find yourself somewhere else to pedal your ideas, time and energy.

We founded our little company on five simple values, one of them being "intelligent risk." That doesn't mean that we would bet the farm for the sake of betting. It means that when a good opportunity or idea comes along, we just may take a chance if it fits our strategic plan and values. History is full of risk takers who bet the farm. Some lost their shirts and their farms.

With big rewards comes big risks and hardly a winner around hasn't a story about a gamble that made the difference.

BUILD TEAMS AND LEADERS

Build teams **and** leaders. We like to say "make every employee a key employee."

At our small restaurant, employees who proved that they loved customers as much as us were made "key" employees and, somewhat symbolically, given a key. Some folks said, "You can't give a key to hourly employees! They might steal something!"

"What do you think they would do? Break in and steal a case of dead, naked chickens?"

If you can't trust an employee with a key to the building, something is wrong. You have the wrong employee. Or, the leadership has failed to create a sense of ownership that would prevent an employee from feeling like an owner.

MAKE INTEGRITY AN ISSUE

Make integrity an issue. If you don't, who will?

I believe that about 5 percent of the population will steal from you given half the chance no matter what you do to include them or reward their contribution. This 5 percent is, in my opinion, pathological. They will get to you if you so much as blink in their presence.

Another 10 percent of the population wouldn't steal or break a rule under any condition. My wife is in that group. If she was being chased by a band of murderers and came upon a "Do not walk on the grass" sign, I am almost certain that she would at least stop to consider her options.

The remaining 85 percent are what I call "situationally honest." They will, for the most part, be pretty good citizens. "They won't take anything...big. Using the office copier to run things for the Little League or copy their tax return, but otherwise, trustworthy. Or, more to the point, easily influenced. Here is where the boss has to set the standard.

Actually, the boss is the standard whether consciously or not.

Here is where we get back to being a quality fanatic which also relates to practicing total integrity. If the product isn't perfect, can you really charge full price? Can you give a half-hearted performance and invoice for the full amount? I think not. Quality is included in the price.

I've never seen a notice that read, "For a quality product or service, please add 20 percent."

Corporate politics are a special category of integrity...or the lack of it. Politics are played wherever people feel they must jockey for power, where normal communications are stopped. In fact, whenever you see politics being played, look for a stop or blockage in communications. While you're at it, notice that where there is politics, only managers are in charge.

Leaders get out of the office and touch people. They treat team players like part of a constituency that must be sold, loved on and coaxed to be their best.

Managers who make it to the top behave just the opposite. They see little or no need to rub shoulders with the little people who only want to rob their time.

Politics happen when...

> ➤ A "manager" is in charge and there is insufficient communication with the troops to get things decided through normal channels.
> ➤ An insufficiently competent individual has ascended to a level of authority and needs to maintain position.
> ➤ People are left in the dark and begin to speculate.

In a former life, we were left without a leader. The manager left in charge immediately created an inner sanctum where he could be free of prying eyes. He had his windows covered over with paneling and the light fixtures darkened. All that was left was a small grow light necessary to keep the violets alive, just barely.

His next move was to select a liaison, someone who would be part-valet, part-confidant and all-communications filter. "Oh, we had better not tell the boss that...he may get upset."

That was a common refrain. Often the communication would be filtered, leaving out bad news or softening the news, depending on the mood of the boss or the power of the player.

At one time I was sent to work in a small office off-campus and told not to come to the main building unless absolutely unavoidable. I was being hidden but I didn't understand why. I stayed in hiding like a good boy, coming out only when called, usually entering through the back door.

For a while I was given a totally unqualified boss who had been selected because the company was under pressure to look better to the EEOC. When I refused to do his work, they finally relented and removed me from his charge until he further disqualified himself by sexually harassing an entry-level employee.

One day while I was still being hidden, I was asked to present recommendations for restructuring training for the company. I had lots of ideas and little time to prepare. But, prepare I did! My report was far beyond my then–boss who also happened to be the presidential liaison. He asked me to slip in through the back door and present to the division managers who were holding court in the main conference room.

The presentation went fabulously well. The division managers bought the program hook, line and sinker. I couldn't help feeling elated and dreaming of a real office.

Then it happened. I discovered that corporate politics would have nothing of me getting recognition for the program much less an office. While sitting at my boss's secretary's desk to use the telephone, I happened to glance at a memo still in the typewriter.

Have you ever noticed that even when you are not consciously reading a document, if your name is mentioned, it seems to jump right off the page? This is what happened to me.

Of course, there was the added thrill of the bright red strikes across my name everywhere it appeared. Beside each, was the boss's name. Where Scott had proposed such and such, it now had been amended to show that the boss had had a major case of brilliance. Scott, apparently, had not even attended.

Sometimes workers at lower levels than the power elite can't figure how such brazenly offensive behavior can go unnoticed. Well, it doesn't. There is justice and it is certain. What goes around really does come around.

That same boss who stole by potential and took credit for my efforts got his. They all do eventually.

One day just before Christmas, I caught the boss with his head in his hands looking for all the world like a dog that had just been kicked hard for no apparent reason.

"What's the problem?"

"The boss wants to fly to Atlanta on Christmas Day to see stores. He says if the stores are open, people from corporate should be seen working, too. He just doesn't want to spend the day at home."

"So? What's that got to do with you?"

"Where he goes, I go. You know that."

"Yes, but it's Christmas and you have a new baby and all of the family coming from out of state. Just tell him you have other plans. He doesn't need a babysitter on the corporate jet."

"I can't."

"I could."

"That's because you don't know what it's like to be this close to power." As he said those words, he squinted through teary eyes, held thumb and index finger close together and when he got to the word "power," it barely eased past his lips as he spoke it in a reverential whisper.

I did know what it was like to be "this close to power." He didn't.

Integrity. What an issue.

It has been said that the reason that the world doesn't work, (we learned this years ago from an est course,) is that people fail to keep their agreements. Think about any major oops in your life or your organization, and dollars to donuts, you'll see that the root cause was an unkept agreement.

If you have trouble relating to this idea of agreements, think for a moment about the agreements that we make as a part of our bargain with society, even though they may be unwritten. For example, isn't there an agreement that says if I pay you for a day's work, you agree to give me your best? Do we not agree, even though there may not be a written policy, to be loyal to our bosses? And don't we have an obligation, an agreement you could say, to protect those who work and play on our team?

Don't we agree to love and protect our children and do what is best for them even though there is no written agreement? Aren't folks who take government assistance agreeing that they will do whatever possible to make themselves fit for work as soon as possible? Or am I just imagining that the world runs more on unwritten agreements than on laws?

Agreements influence everything we do. This even applies to mechanical things such as equipment breakdowns. Think about it. Believe it!

MAKE WORK FUN

Nobody has said it better than Paul Meunier of Signature Flight Services..."Your job is not the means to a happy life. Your job must be a happy life. We spend too much time for it not to be satisfying and fun."

Are you having fun? Are your team players having fun?

This is a tough one. It's too easy to get caught up in the work of work. Racing to meet deadlines, struggling to encourage the incorrigible, playing politics to get ahead or maybe just stay employed. If that is a pretty fair description of your job, take Freddie Krueger's advice and "Get out!" Life really is too short.

When the folks who manufacture Duck Tape meet their quarterly goals, they invite employees and visitors alike to join them in a brisk swim in the pond at their offices. If you dress for the part, fine. If not, you are encouraged, strongly I'm told, to join them anyway. Now, you have to admit that even if that's not what you call fun, it is definitely different!

Fun won't happen if the boss doesn't let it happen. Fun requires leadership, too.

That same fun-loving CEO who wanted to visit stores on Christmas was invited to attend a division party. It was a cookout on Lake Lanier in Georgia. I'll never forget the sight. There we were, a couple of hundred enthusiastic team players, all pumped up on volleyball and watersports. We tackled a mountain of barbeque ribs, pulling them apart as we sat on the shore laughing and enjoying the moment.

There, seated at a card table brought in for the occasion, eating with the only set of metal eating utensils in sight, sat a figure in a sports coat who had long since forgotten how to play. He wore his sport coat in spite of oppressive heat and humidity. And, not wanting to be too close to the confusion of the moment, he had his table placed twenty or thirty yards further along the shore. Close enough to say that he was there but not really.

There is one company that I believe is founded on the idea of having fun. That's my old friends, Southwest Airlines. On SWA, you are likely to hear flight attendants suggest, "If you are seated next to a child or someone who is just acting like one, put your mask on first..." Now, that's fun.

Or would you count the Silly String war I started in the back of one plane on a flight to New Orleans to play at Mardi Gras? We got to spraying each other, then the flight attendants and finally a few of our fellow passengers voted that "our" section of the plane was for party animals! (Okay, so that was a bit out of character!)

This is the airline where the boss has been spotted dressed as Corporal Klinger in the maintenance hanger at two in the morning. He also dresses as the Easter Bunny on what we assume was Easter! I don't think Herb Kelleher would mind a little Silly String as long as he was given a can, too!

And just what good is fun? People who are having fun are actually more productive then those who are spending their time watching the clock. Can you remember when you were working really hard **and** having a good time? If that was yesterday, then we'll all come to work for you!

Fun happens when...

➤ You are working with people whom you enjoy.
➤ You are doing work that has a visible product or result.
➤ You can see your progress.
➤ You are appreciated for your contribution.
➤ You can see the end of the project.

If this sounds like the ingredients for what our friend Charles Coonradt calls The Game of Work, well isn't that a surprise? (Make sure you read the chapter Shaping Performance.)

ANTICIPATE TOMORROW

Good leaders know where they, and hence (a fine, although seldom used word!) you are going. We're talking more than setting goals although that is definitely a key responsibility of a leader. No, we're talking about actually looking into the future, every day, in an attempt to anticipate what obstacles and opportunities lie ahead for the group.

Good leaders anticipate the changing needs of their customers both traditional and internal. They are ready with a plan often before the need fully develops.

Think of the inventors who were mocked when they unveiled their new developments. The inventors of the computer were nothing more than ahead of their time when they estimated a paltry world demand for mainframes to be no more than twenty-five. Henry Ford felt that the world demand for his Model-T was unlikely to ever exceed a million.

"Ahead of his time," really should be translated to be, "ahead of the customer." New ideas languish initially until the customer finally figures a use for them. Take the personal computer. Initially they were used to replace existing technology. They became "super typewriters", then "word processors" and, only after they had sat underutilized for nearly two decades, personal computers have become instruments of instant communication.

Great leaders look beyond the horizon. They never feel completely safe; they never feel like they have finished.

Today at lunch, we heard Frank Sinatra playing on the house sound system. One of our group said, "That guy must be worth millions. Why doesn't he retire?"

He's not finished. That's why.

To build leaders capable of looking far into the future, get them to begin by looking at least as far as tomorrow or next week. Our favorite question, (let me repeat) is, "What's on your list, today?" When people get into the habit of planning their work and being held accountable for working their plan, they begin to make plans that stretch further and further into the future.

It is said that there are three conditions for happiness: Something to love, something to do, and something to look forward to. If you won't be too critical of the definition of love, you could say that loving has something to do with living beyond yourself.

Asking team players to make and live by plans can actually make them happier. They have something to do that seems to fit into a larger picture, something bigger than themselves and they have something to look forward to.

Donna B. just stopped by to read over my shoulder.

"Do you think that talking about love and looking forward to things is a bit much for a business book?"

"Aren't you the guy who says there isn't much that separates life in general from business when you're doing it right?"

"Well, yes."

"My mother always wanted a red-brick house and a pecan tree."

"Have we changed topics?"

"Listen to me! Every time we went to visit, we heard the story about the red-brick house and pecan tree. We thought she was just getting senile so we humored her and listened to that story over and over again.

"Then one day, we noticed she didn't mention the red-brick house. She forgot, we thought, about the pecan tree. But it wasn't long after that she died. I guess she had given up on the red-brick house and the pecan tree."

When you give team players an opportunity to be part of something larger than themselves...when you get them involved and give them a part to play...when they, too, can see and share in the goal and the progress toward its achievement, work is fun and happy. And if that has no place in business, well, I've always wanted to preach.

MANAGE FIRST, LABOR SECOND

One mistake amateur managers make is to confuse labor with management. Bill Oncken, the great management thinker, said that every job has components that are primary vocational in nature and other components that are management.

Vocational work is any work whose primary value lies in time and labor. Management work, according to Oncken, is work that has, as its primary value, judgment and influence.

It is perfectly okay for any of us to do either. What is not okay is to do one but call it the other.

When I am loading books for shipment, that is not management. I am not using judgment. Put them into a box and tape it. I certainly am not exerting much in the way of influence. Even though that task may be necessary, even important, it just isn't management.

Where new managers get into trouble, and some of us older ones as well, is when we think that we are the best draftsperson or merchandiser or negotiator or whatever and spend our time in the trenches showing the rest of the crew "how this job looks when it's done by a pro."

Don't fool yourself! If you came up through the ranks and still think that you haven't lost your touch at whatever it was that used to be your strong suit, if you're out doing that same thing today, it is because you like to do it. Don't give us the crap that you are still the best and the only one who is qualified to handle this account or this project.

That's bull.

And if it is not bull, then you are a lousy manager because the job of management is to assemble and train a competent team. If you really have to handle the project personally, let's see a hand on the foul. Even if you really are the best whatever, you should go back to that job. Leave it to someone who understands that managers have as one of their first responsibilities to hire and train a competent crew.

Remember, please, that real-estate term, "highest and best use." Not that you are too good to take out the trash. Not that you are too good to swing a mop or answer the phone or any other job in the house. Only that when you are doing vocational work AND not training someone at the same time, you are NOT managing.

Do the right things.

LEAD FROM THE HEART

Lead from the heart. Do the right thing.

There are always opportunities to skate away from who you are. There are millions of times when you can do something that is best for the bottom line but it's not the right thing. Even though you can say, "Nobody would blame me for..."

We're not talking about or to "nobody." I'm talking to you!

And sometimes you have to stand up and be counted. There's a country-western song that says that when people won't stand for something important, they will fall for anything. (The lyric, but not the sentiment, is better than I remember it.)

Sometimes you have to get involved with a promotion that you know won't pay for itself but it's the right thing to do. Sometimes you bend or break an attendance policy because of the circumstance. Sometimes you believe in someone for no sane reason.

A couple of years ago, we had an employee at our restaurant who we learned was the prime suspect in a triple-slaying. Just what you want to round out the team.

We thought long and hard over what to do. We had young female employees, a prime target according to the police official who spoke to us off the record. "He can be extremely violent and he hates women."

"Arrest him."

"We can't. Not enough evidence. But we are going to get him."

"He's been a great employee. The customers love him. We have no reason to fire him."

"Suit yourself, but he's our man. Since you guys have been good to us, we won't arrest him at work."

Small favor!

My brother Stuart was our manager. "What should I do?"

"Don't give him any job that requires handling a knife and keep an eye on him."

We worried and that's putting it mildly. When do the rights of one employee begin to weigh on the safety of the entire crew? What would happen if he is the man, as we had reason to suspect, and someone got hurt? What would be our responsibility? Could we lose our business? What about our reputation?

For weeks and then months, the police followed our employee, often escorting him, lights flashing as he rode his bicycle to work. Stuart called one day and said, "Arrest him or leave him alone." They left him alone but we questioned our own sanity, feeling that in some way we might have stepped over the line in the wrong direction.

One day we heard it on the radio. In a surprise raid stemming from an unexpected break in the case, the killer had been arrested.

It wasn't our man.

We had done the right thing.

Some years earlier, I had hired a sharp new team member to take over our national training center. He knew his business and had performed admirably while running one of our division centers. No reason to think that he wouldn't do well with the promotion.

Within weeks, we were beginning to suspect our decision. His behavior went from even-tempered professional to borderline bizarre.

I sent him to a doctor where he was treated for stress and depression.

Gee, that seemed oddly out of character for this man I was certain that I knew well.

Within a few more weeks of even further deteriorating behavior, I found myself standing on the plush carpet of the Chairman of the Board.

"Scott, I don't understand why you haven't gotten rid of this guy. He's just not capable. If you allow this to persist, it will be your judgment that will be questioned."

"Sorry, sir. I don't know what is the problem but I know it's not what you think."

I sent our man packing for a second medical opinion.

Two weeks later, I was back in the Chairman's office but not feeling all that popular.

"Scott, I think one of us is going to have to make a move."

"I won't fire him. You can fire me first. I know that I'm right."

"One week."

Outside the office, I felt that I was walking right on the edge. I had visions of job and family, house and friends, all going up in smoke over the lousy notion of principle, over a guy who was probably just too weak-willed to buck up and do his job.

Nooo!

"Come on."

"Where are we going?"

"To find you a neurosurgeon."

"Why?"

"To save your job. Mine, too."

"Mr. Gross, I'm glad you brought your friend in. We're going to have to tap into that thick skull of his right away and see if we can't relieve a little pressure. He wants to wait until Monday so that he can get ahead of things at the office. He says he's one of your key employees. But to tell you like it is, if we don't get to him right away, I doubt that he will be with us as long as Monday. Hope you don't mind losing a key man for a few days."

They removed eighty-four cc's of fluid from his cerebral cavity. They saved his life.

Saved my job, too! And taught me a lesson. When you have a choice and it doesn't seem clear, listen to your gut and do the right thing.

BREAK THE RULES, HONOR THE VALUES

Break the rules, honor the values. It will never happen. Unless, of course, if you have a set of values that support rule-breaking.

Let's have a corollary commandment:

First mistakes, if they benefit the customer, are free.

Employees who expect to be chopped into small pieces if they make a mistake, will never make a mistake...they won't do anything. You can always tell operations where first mistakes are often last mistakes — team players do as little as possible and spend as much effort trying to cover their anatomy as they do at their actual work.

One, often overlooked cause of low productivity, is office politics, which are often bred by an atmosphere where mistakes can be suicidal. We tend to think that it is politics that discourage intelligent risk-taking. Not necessarily so. Sometimes it is exactly the other way around.

People realize that leadership (poor word for this example) is so afraid of screwing up that the rest of the crew has to have a scapegoat in waiting, just in case.

THE NEW LEADER, SKILLS AND VALUES

The new leader will, above all else, be a change master. This is an unavoidable requirement in a world where change is the operating force of the day. Bill Gates of Microsoft talks about the developing world being nearly 100 percent connected to the information superhighway by as early as 1997. Think what that can mean to an economy and even our way of life.

The manner in which business is both organized and conducted is about to be turned upside down. Changing technology is bringing nothing short of a revolution to our world.

How we respond to this revolution, or fail to respond, will make all the difference. Some folks will stand on the sidelines, content to let more adventurous business leaders fight the battles and conquer new territory. Others will rush to the head of the ranks. They will, perhaps, take the biggest risks. On the other hand, they will be first to divide the spoils.

What makes this revolution unusual is that it may not have an end. That means that today's winners could easily become tomorrow's casualties. Change can be salvation or defeat in a world moving at the speed of an electron.

The winners will be those who learn to, if not love change, at least take advantage of it. It will take a new sort of aggression to lead the organization of tomorrow. Leaders will have to do something that few are comfortable doing; they will have to learn to give up pride of authorship; they will learn not to become attached to ideas and processes; they will learn not to depend even on their own technical skills in a world where skills, like the technology they represent, are quickly and regularly driven into obsolescence.

Hewlett-Packard, creators of the world's most successful line of black-and-white printers for office computers, is racing to invent a new breed of color printers. And what competitor has the product-development team targeted? Why, Hewlett-Packard, of course! If they are successful, the new product will no doubt make their current line of black-and-white machines obsolete.

"You have to attack yourself before the competition does," says H-P leadership. Pretty gutsy to attack the world's biggest and best, particularly if that happens to be you!

The new leader will be a master of reinvention.

Motorola is another company both on and under attack. Motorola dominates the world market in cellular telephones. Remember those little instruments that only a few years ago were symbols of bourgeois decadence? Today Motorola has what is easily the lion's share of the market. Their ISO 9000 production standards and aggressive marketing tactics have enabled Motorola to beat the pants off the competition.

Now, Motorola is preparing to beat the pants off Motorola. The latest projects will create a satellite-based communications system that, when implemented, will make the cellular phone as we know it today, a thing of the past. "Hello, Smithsonian?"

2

CHEERS!

If the picture that is unfolding looks suspiciously like that of the Renaissance Leader, so be it. The new leader will have to be more than a technological innovator; the new leader will have to create or borrow ideas rapidly, immediately setting about the task of selling them to the team.

The new leader will be an ace cheerleader, not just motivating for more of the same but selling ideas and the changes that are part and parcel to their adoption.

New leaders create an emotional acceptance.

The days when new ideas could be issued as directives straight from the Puzzle Palace, are, for most organizations, gone. In the new organization, there will be fewer middle managers to enforce their implementation.

New ideas must, more than ever, be sold by management and bought by the team. No buy-in? No implementation. And what change is made, may come so slowly as to be of little consequence.

A recent *Wall Street Journal* article reported that an internal survey of top managers revealed that 40 percent of them still don't "accept the need for change." Really?

Whether you are IBM or Smith's Corner Store, there is now a need for change. And that need isn't going to go away. It's going to grow!

Once the idea of change is on the burner, great leaders anchor that change in the form of celebration and new tradition. What could you do?

List the things that you could celebrate that would anchor change in your organization.

Here's our list...

> First anniversary of the Technology Application Team.
> The first, tenth or even one hundredth revamped store.
> The one-thousandth employee suggestion.
> Whenever a piece of technology becomes obsolete, have it, or a portion of it, bronzed and given to the person who originally used it or brought it to the company.
> Celebrate new ideas by inviting players who contribute suggestions to an event in their honor.
> Celebrate media coverage that is positive and involves new technology, products or services.

Sitting in a small cafe in Los Angeles with one of our new hires, he noticed first that everyone seemed to be eating healthy food. He remarked that there was no one smoking, even in the outdoor eating area where smoking was permitted. A few minutes into our meal, which was breakfast right before a scheduled video shoot, he observed that the patrons appeared to be well-off in spite of the fact that most were in jogging or other types of exercise clothes.

"It must be nice to have enough bucks that all you have to do is hang out at trendy cafes," he said.

A few minutes later, he noticed that while everyone looked relaxed and healthy, nearly everyone in the place was reading a book or journal or working over a set of documents.

"Maybe I was wrong about these people. They all seem to be working. They all seem to be well-off...and healthy. Who are these people?"

They were the new leaders. Today's successful leader doesn't even look like the leaders of a decade ago.

The new leader is...

Well-read

A non-smoker

A moderate or non-drinker

Multi-dimensional

Values-oriented

Health-conscious

An early riser

Flexible

Goal-oriented

In other words, the new leader is a whole person attempting to lead a whole company.

The new leader has to be that way because, in a changing world, managers who fail to look at the organization as a complete organism in a symbiotic relationship with its market and its economy, will undoubtedly fail. When you begin to see relationships on a grand scale, it's nearly impossible not to have the same vision of self.

The only survivors in a rapidly changing world will be those who have developed a keen awareness of that world. Always looking over the horizon, always looking out, enables you to bring a whole lot of information home.

The new leader is nothing if not well-informed. This is, after all, the information age and it stands to reason that those most likely to prosper will have to be among the most and best informed.

Russ Umphenor (we'll meet him in a few pages) is a voracious reader, subscribing to dozens of periodicals and devouring even more when he's on the road. Asked why he reads so many — even magazines targeted at women and ethnic minorities — he says, "I have to know what my customers know. I have to know what my customers think."

The new leader is more than a consumer of news, he or she is a black hole for any tidbit of data that intersects their wide orbit.

In the past few years, the trend has become undeniable...the poor smoke and drink. The new leaders avoid such vices as though they were the plague. Couch potatoes don't live in big houses, they work in them.

The new leader is, if not a health nut, certainly health-conscious. I can't remember speaking at a conference or seminar where smoking was either tolerated or practiced by more than a few. I see even banquet menus being designed with health in mind. More and more you will see the top executives push away from the desserts, skip the butter and go light on the dressing. That's just the way it is.

The new leader is no longer a one-dimensional character who lives solely for the company store and expects the employees to do and feel the same. The new leader is as likely to attend an opera as a baseball game, perhaps both in the same day.

If you want to speak to the new leader, call early before the secretary arrives to intercept the call. Leaders are almost always early risers.

Mary K. Ash, founder of Mary Kay Cosmetics, is famous for accepting members into her Five O'clock Club. (No, we're not talking p.m.!) Join the club and you become fair game for a phone call anytime after 5 a.m.

That's no surprise. Leaders aren't married to the time clock as are traditional workers. As the trend to work at home continues, we will begin to see the nation's sleeping habits change. The boss will still get up early but soon she will have a whole lot more company. It will be a sign of status to attend early morning meetings.

We met the first two times with the folks at Federal Express at 7 a.m. breakfasts. At our POSSE events (Positively Outrageous Sales and Service Experience), we often serve breakfast immediately following a brisk walk that steps off at 6:30 a.m.

As we become connected to the information superhighway, the time and place of meetings will become less relevant. And casual dress will become the rule rather than the exception. If you are working at home all day, why would you want to dress for the day's only outside meeting?

The most important traits of the new leaders may very well be the push-pull personality characteristics of flexibility and goal orientation.

The new leader must be flexible about everything except the goal.

How will the inflexible survive in a world where computers are bring us the capability to be more flexible than ever? We can be flexible about the time and place of meetings; more flexible about how documents are arranged, printed and stored; more flexible in terms of how a product or service is created. In a world that is, oh, so flexible, the new leader must be the most flexible of all...yet keep an unwavering eye on the goal.

TIME OUT

If a leader is to be as flexible as we say, how in the world will the new leader ever get anything done?

The best leaders make flexibility, in terms of how they use their time, an advantage. While the rest of the world must focus on the next customer or the next assembly along the line, leaders are not required to be so focused. They are focused but in a different sort of way. They literally jump from one project to the next, barely lighting on one before taking off for the next.

Great leaders are managing their time as a series of interruptions, taking advantage of each to sell an idea or add their special input. These leaders use small bursts of attention to enable them to touch as many people and projects as possible.

Studies show that the average top executive rarely spends more than two hours each day doing something that was preplanned. The rest is one interruption after another. Stephanie Winston in *The Organized Executive* says, "Interrupted work doesn't distract from executive work. It is executive work."

Harry Mintzberg studied executive time use and learned that a surprising 49 percent of executive time is spent in short bursts that typically last less than nine minutes and that only a spare 10 percent of executive time is spent in activities that last more than an hour. Short attention? Sounds like executive material to me!

If interruptions are the bulk of an executive's day, isn't it a wonder that they get anything done? Not really. Interruptions can actually save time for both the executive and others. Think about how much faster it is to verbally deliver a message than to write, read and file a memo. And for the executive, who no doubt is being approached for either advice or approval, look at the time saved in the reply.

Besides, executives, those who are truly leaders, rarely give direct orders. The new leader is first a salesperson, packaging ideas and selling them to the troops for maximum buy-in. Who needs to give orders when a team player who is sold will act on her own and fill in the blanks when unexpected situations arise?

That's not to say that the new leader is a wimp. Louis Gerstner, Jr., new chief of IBM, is quoted as having told his troops, "You should decide if you want to be here. If you don't, leave." Kind of a "buy or die" sentiment.

Even the easy-to-love Paul Meunier of Signature Flight Services has stern advice for nonbelievers. He has been known to tell his players, "...if you think that you've seen it all, if you think that the conventional wisdom, the old ways, the time-tested and proved methods, are the best, do yourself a favor and use this valuable time to update your resume. Don't walk. Run for the door."

The new leader may be a salesperson but when it is clear that their efforts are leading to an unspoken, "No sale," they have a very new age way to respond..."Next!"

Gerstner of IBM took on the old values of Big Blue and attempted to give them new life. Old man Watson left the company with three key principles and the admonition to be willing to change everything, "except these basic beliefs." And along comes an outsider who wants to do just the opposite.

Watson's top three were, "pursue excellence, provide the best customer service and above all, show employees respect for the individual."

Gerstner came up with a list of eight. But he is dealing with an entrenched, highly patriarchal organization. It may be that if things don't change and change soon, he will have to add a ninth..."Next!"

Jack Welch of General Electric has a similar twist but a slightly different challenge. He, according to the *Wall Street Journal*, divides his internal sales prospects into four categories...

➤ Those who produce as well as support the values MUST be promoted.

➤ Those who produce but don't support the values MUST hit the road.

➤ Those who neither produce nor support the values MUST hasta la vista.

➤ Those who fail to produce but do support the values MUST be given a second chance.

Welch says that in an age where good ideas are needed from everyone in the organization, neither he nor GE can afford to tolerate management styles that suppress and intimidate.

(Notice please, that when it comes to setting priorities, the new leader will spend time with those who are riding the same train but seem to have little or no use for hangers-on who are looking for a free ride to an unscheduled stop.)

When do our new leaders find time for strategic thinking and planning? Look closer, that's exactly what they are doing as they conduct those mini-bursts of interactions with customers and staff. They are constantly revising their personal strategic plan as they go!

To sum up the new leader and the world in which they will do business, here's a list of trends, composed in a style I learned from the infinitely eloquent Meunier...

What's In?	**What's Out?**
Doers	Overseers
Leaders	Managers (bosses)
Taking responsibility	Placing blame
Selling	Telling
Computer fluent	Computer illiterate
Global thinking	Xenophobia

...and the new leader will be a revolutionary!

What's In?	**What's Out?**
Eye on technology	Rooted to old methods
Anticipates changing customer needs	Looks for new customers

Organized around a goal	Organized around a product
Focused goals, shared	Muddled goals, decreed
Teamwork with individual responsibility	Individual work
Emphasis on culture and tradition	Sacred cows
Partnership with players and customers	Top-down buyer/seller relationships
Learning and renewal	That's the way we've always done it
Valued diversity	Homogeneous workforce
Meaningful work	Feed the system
People-centered technologies	Product first, safety and comfort second
Balanced stakeholder interests	Company always first

BALDRIGE...

In 1987, the U.S. Congress created an unusual public-private alliance, supported by the Foundation for the Malcolm Baldrige National Quality Award Foundation..

Baldrige was Secretary of Commerce from 1981 until his death in 1987. The award is intended to promote U.S. leadership in product and process quality.

The Baldrige Award is, in fewest words, a quality audit. Participant's businesses are evaluated in seven performance areas, the first of which is leadership.

How does Baldrige evaluate leadership? By answering these questions...

➤ Are senior executives personally involved in developing and maintaining an environment that promotes quality excellence?

➤ Do they create and reinforce customer focus and quality values?

➤ Are they involved in setting expectations and planning?

➤ Are they involved in reviewing quality and operational performance?

➤ Do they personally recognize employee contributions?

➤ Do they communicate quality values outside the company? (This may include the media, national and state industry organizations.)

➤ How are customer focus and quality values integrated into day-to-day leadership?

➤ What are the principle roles communicated by senior leadership to management and supervision as related to quality?

➤ How are the company's quality values and customer focus communicated throughout the entire workforce?

➤ How is overall performance and quality reviewed throughout the organization?

➤ How are managers' and supervisors' effectiveness at reinforcing quality values and customer focus evaluated?

➤ How does the company meet its responsibilities to the public in its quality policies and improvement practices?

➤ How does the company lead as a corporate citizen?

➤ How does the company consider risks, regulatory and legal requirements in setting operational requirements and targets?

➤ How does the company anticipate public concerns and the impact of its products, services and operations on the public?

➤ How does the company promote legal and ethical conduct in all that it does?

➤ How has the company responded to any sanctions received under law, regulation, or contact?

Where do you stand? If the Baldrige Award committee, or even *60 Minutes*, showed up on your doorstep, how would you fare in a surprise audit of your corporate leadership?

Read on to meet a few interesting leaders that would do very well!

3

MORE POSITIVELY
OUTRAGEOUS SERVICE

You write a book and think that you know everything. Funny thing about good ideas; they have many authors and there are more than the expected reasons that make them ideas whose time has come. The longer I preach about Positively Outrageous Service, the more people I meet who say, "Oh, we've been doing that for years," or, "Gee, thanks for giving us a name to pin on the way we've always done business."

I've met people like Phil Romano, restaurateur and showman, who has been wowing customers forever with his offbeat brand of showmanship. And there is Southwest Airlines, the little airline that could...and then did...that has been making customers feel like owners since the first flight took off not that many years ago.

We've seen a jillion small deeds done on behalf of customers, good business and just plain friendly behavior. We've heard about, but not had the opportunity to read what must be a wonderful book called *Random Acts of Kindness*. I'd like to think that they got the idea from us but, the truth is, the truth is. And good ideas don't really have owners any more than a farmer can take credit for the rain. Random Acts of Kindness seems to be the personal side of POS. Still, Positively Outrageous Service has been an idea that has captured the attention of business people everywhere. From hardware stores to airlines, ophthalmologists to bellmen, POS is the weapon of choice for hundreds of thousands of smart operators everywhere.

What have we learned since *Positively Outrageous Service* was first published in 1991?

During the media tour for POS, we were surprised at the number of times people asked, "How do I get Positively Outrageous Service?" Didn't everybody get good service?

In 1992, we wrote the customer version of POS and called it simply enough, *How to Get What You Want From Almost Anybody.*

We gave our readers four simple tactics for putting themselves on the receiving end of POS. The tactics are, just in case you want to know:

Recognize the power relationship...the clerk has it, not the customer.

Ask for exactly what you want...that includes asking for nonstandard items and, remember, if the clerk were psychic, he would have a better job!

Market yourself...to the clerk, you're just another pretty face. Do something to stand out.

Reward great service...people do the things that get rewarded, so reward!

By 1993, we had discovered that some folks practice POS so regularly that we had to give their brand a whole new name. That year we wrote *Positively Outrageous Service and Showmanship.* Showmanship consists of the little things that you do as part of your SOP, (standard operating procedures) that give your product or service a unique personality...yours!

And we are still learning.

WHAT DO YOU EXPECT!

We now realize that one of the great dangers of Positively Outrageous Service is mismanaged expectations.

What is the definition of the best service, POS, that you've ever had? It was: Random and unexpected; out-of-proportion to the circumstance; the customer was highly involved; and the result was compelling word-of-mouth.

Now, here's a little test: What is the definition of the **worst** service that you ever had?

Surprise! It was random and unexpected, out-of-proportion to the circumstance, the customer was highly involved and the result was compelling word-of-mouth. Get it? The definition of the best service, Positively Outrageous Service, is exactly the same as the definition of the worst service, plain old outrageously awful service.

How do you account for the difference? Simple. It's a matter of expectations.

If I promised you pretty good product at a pretty good price and I pretty well deliver it, what's to talk about? You only feel compelled to tell the world when I promise pretty good and deliver something less. You even talk when I deliver pretty good if the promise was for something substantially more.

A couple who paid $1,800 per person per day for a cruise returned to the travel agent and gave her holy hell. Why? Because for $1,800 per person per day, the room steward should have remembered to replace the soap daily, that's why!

Where we have seen our clients get into trouble with their experimentation with POS is in the mismanagement of customer expectations. Putting up a sign that says, "Positively Outrageous Service Practiced Here" may make this writer feel good, but in terms of customer expectations, you are shooting yourself in the foot.

I tell the story about a department store where the concierge noticed a car had run out of gas in front of the store. He raced into traffic and pushed the car to the curb, telling the driver that since traffic was so heavy and someone should stay with the car, he would go for a tank of gas.

Upon returning, he filled the tank, patted the car on the fender and smiled at the driver saying, "Thanks for driving by our store...no charge!"

I would call that POS. It was random and unexpected service. It was out-of-proportion to the circumstance and it definitely created compelling word-of-mouth. Where the department store management went wrong was when they took out a newspaper ad and ran a radio commercial telling the world about the great service delivered by their concierge.

Unfortunately, all this managed to do was to artificially raise customer expectations. Now what do people in the neighborhood do when they are low in gas? Circle the department store!!

TAKES TWO TO TANGIBLE!

One consistent service problem that we have seen over the past few years is that, while many of our clients have become masters at giving great, even Positively Outrageous Service, they are terrible at telling the customer. It's the marketing of your service that gives it value beyond the service itself.

In our restaurant days, I took great pains to tell our customers about how we cut and marinated our chicken. We told them that it arrived fresh, never frozen and that we cut every piece by hand immediately after we had marinated it for a full twenty-two hours. That was the reason why our chicken had great flavor in every bite...we marinated to get the flavor all the way to the bone, not just in the breading.

One day while having lunch in my dining room, I overheard two gentlemen.

"This," said the first, as he smacked his lips and sat back to enjoy the bite he had just taken, "is the best tasting chicken that I have ever put in my mouth. Mmmm, it's absolutely deeelicious!"

"It oughta be. They marinate this stuff for almost twenty-four hours!"

Point: Service that the customer is not aware of is no service at all. Or, more accurately, service that the customer is not aware of has no value. For service to have value, the customer must know about it.

Do this...

Look for opportunities to tell your customer about your service, especially service that he may not see or experience directly.

Could you put information about value-added service on the price tag or on or near the display? Could you put something in your product brochure or on employee name tags? Are there special licensing or training requirements that your employees must meet in order to serve your customers that would be regarded as an added value if the customer knew about them? Do you take extra steps to ensure quality or freshness or reliablity that would enhance the perceived value?

Marketing is not an activity that should be isolated from the sales transaction.

One to One

There is an important new book, *The One to One Future* by Peppers and Rogers, that reminds us of another reason why Positively Outrageous Service is an idea whose time has come. Peppers and Rogers offer the idea that the new marketer will realize that it is just as important to be concerned with customer share as it is to fight for market share.

In a few words, they say that it is much cheaper to hold on to the customers that you already have and sell them more than it is to go looking for fresh customers after each and every sale. That is increasing your share of customer, getting a larger portion of each customer's business potential.

Peppers and Rogers have some interesting ideas and compelling arguments for their vision of The One to One Future where relationship marketing will be the rule of the day for those who are among the most successful.

Well, what do you think is Positively Outrageous Service if it's not rela-tionship marketing in its purest form? No fancy database required, other than you and me, eyeball to eyeball, establishing a temporary but often highly personal relationship that exists for but a few seconds yet cements your loyalty to my product or service as fast as fast can be.

RANDOM

The single, most important idea behind Positively Outrageous Service is the concept of surprise. The one word that goes hand in hand with POS is random. The instant that an action becomes predictable, it ceases to be a surprise. Instead it is an expectation.

It is okay to have a reputation for surprising the customer with out-of-proportion service actions so long as the actions themselves are not pre-dictable. Once the actions become predictable, all you have managed to do is raise the bar on what now constitutes great service.

MANAGING EXPECTATIONS

We manage our customer's service expectations in countless, often un-suspected ways.

Think about the times you have been in a business and seen those car-toon signs where the characters are rolling with laughter under the cap-tion, "You want it when?" Shapes your expectations, doesn't it?

Or how about when you arrive at a restaurant and are greeted by the owner who calls you by name? How do you feel when you arrive at a hotel and they can't find your reservations? Again, something small has happened to shape your expectations.

Shaping customer expectations often creates poor customer behavior.

Customers may tear into you with both guns blazing when they want to make a simple exchange. You wonder, "What bee got in his bonnet?" Look behind you at the sign that says, "No refunds or exchanges without a receipt. No cash refunds. No refunds after thirty days." The customer has an expectation that the only way to get a refund is to be prepared to fight. You did it, not the customer.

The folks at The Spaghetti Warehouse have printed on their menu that they will limit the number of drinks that will be served. Shapes your ex-pectation that this is a pretty nice place to eat and that rowdy customers won't be a problem.

"Exact Fare Only" says, "Don't bother us by asking for change."

An airplane that is oven-hot while passengers are boarding makes them wonder if the plane will take off on schedule. If the temperature is pleasant upon boarding, the expectation is that everything is just fine, thank you.

Smell something good in the kitchen and your expectation is a whole lot different than when the counter is littered with boxes that held microwavable meals.

When the telephone is answered by a human, a pleasant how-can-I-help-you type, your expectation is night and day compared to when you are greeted by "For marketing, press one..."

Do this...

Immediately walk through your operation to see how you can shape customer expectations, from how the phone is answered to the quality of your correspondence. From minor policy to pricing policy. From exterior to rest room. What are you doing, what hidden messages are you sending that shape customer expectations?

Absolutely, Positively

You have to get up pretty early to out-POS the master...but that's exactly what the good people of Federal Express Customer Service did when I keynoted to their annual customer service seminar in Williamsburg, Va. Each attendee had received a copy of POS several weeks before the event and took to heart the suggestion that they read the book before arriving in Virginia. (Boy, does that make a difference in the audience's understanding of the concept!)

Peggy Gaston of Federal Express corporate had what I think is the most fun-touching-personal idea ever. A copy of POS was put on the registration table and each attendee was invited to autograph the book. Now there's a twist! Usually I am the one doing the signing! I was presented with this wonderful gift...nearly 400 signatures, many listing their home locations from around the world. Many of the signers chose a page or chapter that was especially important to them while quite a few made comments explaining why.

Random, unexpected, out-of-proportion to the circumstance and, definitely, it's the story that I can't wait to tell!

TIME TO MAKE THE DONUTS!

At Federal Express Customer Service in Sacramento, a wonderful manager-cum-pastry chef has created a unique way to demonstrate the Positively Outrageous Service concept to new hires. Chef Virgil and crew don toques and tuxedos and prepare a delightful welcome feast for new employees.

Talk about serving those that serve! This is a delicious way to make the point!

M-I CROOKA LETTER I

Can you spell Mississauga? Canada, that is!

Good friend and avid practitioner of POS, Andy Thomas, called to send a copy of POS to an associate that he felt would enjoy joining the POS fraternity. In the process, he shared a story that could only be described as "tableside marketing."

Andy stopped at the Airport Ramada Inn near Toronto International to try the buffet. Andy had heard rave reviews and wanted a first-hand experience. Just inside the door, Andy was greeted by a polite, young man who said, "Welcome to our buffet. Please allow me to show you our fine selection." Andy said that at each section of the buffet, the gentleman stopped to point out his favorite, speaking with a definite oriental accent. At the entree section, the description was, "...and our roast beef, sooo tender, sooo juicy!" Andy couldn't resist.

When employees take the time to add their own bit of personality, every transaction can become an experience!

ADIA MAKES THE DAY!

Tracey Moreno wrote to share her delight with Patrice Zeitz with Adia Personnel Services in Austin, Texas. Patrice has been known to call her job placements at 3 a.m. to be sure they won't miss an early shift! Now that's POS!

WHAT GOES AROUND...

If what goes around really does come around, then Cathleen Frazier of Dallas, Texas, will live on Main Street in Heaven! Recently an article in the *Dallas Morning News* told of the plight of an inner city resident who had made it her life work to care for neighborhood children who had been abandoned or left as latchkey children. The article reported that the woman was in dire need of clothes washing facilities.

Cathleen immediately arranged for Sears to deliver a top of the line washer-dryer combination. Then she telephoned to find out what type of detergent the lady preferred and had a large supply of that delivered also.

Would you call that POS? I'd call it VSP...Very Special Person!

TYPE-RIGHTER

Change is a funny thing. People don't really resist change for the sake of being recalcitrant. They just want to hang onto their position, their place of comfort whether that's physical, financial, personal or social.

When Mom came to work for us in the office, we didn't quite know how things might work out. After all, I had spent forty years saying "Yes, Ma'am, " and I didn't quite know how she would take to the slightly different relationship.

I should have been more worried about Mom making an adjustment to the idea of working with modern office equipment. I invited her to spend the first week working with the tutorial that came with our contact management software, which formed the heart of our operation.

After a week had passed, I brought her a handwritten memo that I had scribbled out on the plane and asked to put her tutorial time to the test. After what seemed like a very long time, Mom came out of the office, put her hands on her hips, (a Mom's way of showing that she meant business), stomped her little foot and said, "What kind of office do you call this? You don't even have a typewriter. I can't work this computer nonsense. This can just wait until tomorrow when I can bring in my Selectric (typewriter)!"

"Mom, we use a computer. It can do a million things that your Selectric couldn't begin to manage. Please just gut it out. You'll see."

About a month later, the hard drive died.

When Mom came into work and discovered that the computer was down, she stormed out of her office, put her hands on her hips to show that she meant business, stomped her little foot and said, "What kind of an office do you call this, anyway? How do you expect me to get anything done without my computer!"

HUGS

You can get a Hershey Kiss, a Hershey "Hugs and Kisses," and, if you stay at the Hotel Hershey, you may even be the recipient of a Hershey

Hotel Hug. Actually, the hotel version isn't something to eat although it is sweet to the traveler who may have seemingly unresolvable problems.

At the Hershey Hotel, H.U.G.S. is an acronym for Hershey Understands Guest Service and is an invitation to the traveler to call a special hotline for any problem that doesn't seem resolvable through regular channels.

If that isn't enough to sell you on the Hershey Hotel, maybe the "Comeback Guarantee" will convince you that your stay is bound to be perfect. According to the guarantee, if you are unsatisfied for any reason, other than due to rules required for safety, your return visit will be on the house as long as you take the time to tell the management the reason for your dissatisfaction.

I didn't want to steal the announcement card so I could report on H.U.G.S. verbatim, but you get the idea...stay at Hershey, get Kisses, Hugs and Kisses and a guaranteed Positively Outrageous Service experience!

A Wing and a Thigh

The story comes second or third hand. That's the way it is with legends. People love to repeat them. Positively Outrageous Service is the stuff of which service legends are made.

It seems that at the Atlanta Marriott, before it became the Marriott Marquis, traveling sports teams were especially fond of the fried chicken. For one reason or another, one franchise decided to switch to the hotel across the street. What the team hated the most was the loss of that wonderful fried chicken. So, one night, they called Marriott room service and ordered fried chicken which was promptly delivered by a heads-up Marriott employee.

The legend continues to recount that the employee was later honored with the Willard Marriott Award of Excellence. I guess Marriott understands very well, the value of rewarding Positively Outrageous Service no matter where it occurs!

P.S....some years later I watched a huge convention group attempt to simultaneously register at the Marriott-now-Marquis. The desk staff was unable to handle such a huge group which soon turned surly at the prospect of having to wait to check in. A sharp assistant manager suddenly appeared followed by several waiters bearing huge trays of fresh fruit and juices. Instantly what had moments before been a mob turned into a party. Only a few wanted to be bothered when it was finally their turn to check in!

ALL IN THE NAME

At a trade show, a bright young man stopped at our booth to inquire what was Positively Outrageous Service. When we explained, he simply said, "Oh! I do that!" as he handed us his business card. It was a card from Applebee's Neighborhood Grill and Bar. On the face of it, he had written, "Ask for Vince."

His title? "Tableside gourmet food consultant and public relations representative."

And he really was!

WINDOWS

The dress was beautiful. It called to him from the window of a small Cincinnati dress shop. But the businessman had meetings to attend and planes to catch, no time for anything that wasn't strictly business. But the dress was beautiful as was his wife who would look "just right" if only the shop were open. It would be a surprise. Something perfect for his partner of twenty-five years. In a day or two, they would attend a lavish affair at the exclusive Broadmoor in Colorado Springs.

He decided to wait until the store reopened even though it would mean missing his plane and getting in much too late for comfort. But then, the dress and its wearer were special and worth the inconvenience.

Maybe the evening was truly special. More likely it was a matter of two best friends and great lovers just being together.

You can learn about POS from surprising sources. Thanks, Dad!

SHARING SHERATON

When I checked into the Sheraton in Lansing, Mich., it was immediately obvious that the general manager, Cindy, had read POS and taken it to heart. She, along with the Convention and Visitors Bureau's Mary Katherine, had peppered my room with POS starting with this welcome note...

"...we hope that you will find our facilities and services notable, and our employees cordial, willing, and maybe, a little outrageous!" (I did and they were!)

In the bathroom, a bottle of "Outrageous Shampoo" was at the sink. A goodie basket was on the table, a few well-chosen books near the bed and, smiling at me from the bureau was a framed photo of my wife and me! Now that's Positively Outrageous Service!

PART VII

MANAGER'S TOOLBOX

1

TEAM MANAGEMENT DIAGNOSTIC

Employees work hard but not together.
   Why...

➤ There is no sense of team...we didn't think to work together.
➤ Players distrust one another.
➤ Job is organized so as to discourage teamwork.

   Look for...

➤ Opportunities to create teams charged with completing specific projects.
➤ Politics and gossip that may be breeding mistrust.
➤ Reward systems that promote individual performance.

   Do...

➤ Begin to assign interesting projects to teams of team players.
➤ Refuse to tolerate third-party communication. Require speakers to include the third party in the conversation.
➤ Examine the reward systems and make certain that there is a strong incentive for working as a team.

Employees work hard but produce poor results.
   Why...

➤ Goals are not clearly stated to those involved.
➤ The production system doesn't support the desired outcomes.
➤ Employees are not working as teams.

Look for...

➤ False goals that may have been tacitly encouraged by management.

➤ Faults in work design that may be working against goal achievement.

➤ Rewards that may be promoting counterproductive individual work.

Do...

➤ Clarify goals or set new goals.

➤ Help team members set daily objectives.

➤ Provide frequent feedback on progress to goal.

➤ Review the job process and correct flaws of policy, procedure and physical operation that may be counterproductive.

➤ Review the reward system, including informal social feedback and restructure or focus to promote teamwork.

Political in-fighting and gossip.

Why...

➤ There is always a reward or perceived reward for any behavior including anti-social behavior.

Look for...

➤ Unrecognized, probably informal, reward systems that reward back-stabbing.

➤ Gossipers who may be working just at or even below the level of performance required of their job.

Do...

➤ Cease to listen to or otherwise participate in gossip.

➤ Require, if there is to be criticism of a third party, that party must be present.

➤ Create a policy that states that gossip is viewed as not-team play and make it known that politicians will be invited to play for another team.

Teams produce erratically.

Why...

➤ Erratic performance is almost always due to misunderstood goals.

Look for...

➤ Unclear goals.

➤ Random changes in equipment.

➤ Possible consistent poor performance in one product or service area that might give the appearance that overall performance is erratic.

➤ Erratic presence of a conflicting goal or motivator.

Do...

➤ Graph performance to help pinpoint when and where it varies.

➤ Look for opportunities to clarify goals.

➤ Provide frequent feedback on performance.

High Absenteeism.

Why...

➤ People don't miss things that are fun on purpose. Absenteeism is frequently higher on Fridays and Mondays as employees stretch out their weekends.

Look for...

➤ Cycles in the work routine that correlate with absenteeism.

➤ Rewards or disincentives that may correlate with absenteeism.

➤ Opportunities to make work more like the weekend...fun.

Do...

➤ Eliminate disincentives.

➤ Create incentives...i.e., randomly reward, in some fashion, folks who are present during periods associated with high absenteeism.

➤ Review the job design and build in opportunities for creativity and judgment; eliminate boring routine.

Excellent product; sales are down.

Why...

➤ Just because you think things are fine doesn't mandate that the customer agrees.

Look for...

➤ Unexpected new products or prices from your competition that make your product or service seem less attractive to your customer.

➤ Possible defects, real or imagined, that make your product less desirable.

Do...

➤ Ask, verbally or via survey, why and how purchasing patterns have changed.

➤ Look for correlations between production changes and sales.

➤ Look for correlations between sales and changes in the marketplace or to your customer base.

Lack of customer loyalty.

Why...

➤ Customer loyalty is not a given; it must be earned.

Look for...

➤ Reasons why your customer should be loyal to you or others.

➤ Ways to develop a relationship between you and your customer.

Do...

➤ Create a frequent-customer program.

➤ Initiate regular communications to your customer, even when they are not buying.

➤ Look for opportunities to deliver POS...and get started!

Advertising does not produce results.

Why...

➤ Four things have to happen for advertising to work. It must be: Desirable, Exclusive, Believable and Convenient. If all four of those conditions are not met in the right combinations for your market, no amount of advertising will work.

➤ Advertising must also be received by the right audience and the timing must be perfect.

Look for...

➤ Other advertising that had captured your customer's attention.

➤ Details about your offer that do not match the target.

➤ Insufficient reach and frequency...not enough people hear the message with a frequency great enough to matter.

Do...

➤ Ask your customers where else they shop and why.

➤ Research to define your target.

➤ Refine your offer and format to match the target.

➤ Focus your efforts, even if it means fewer campaigns and media outlets.

Low productivity in spite of hard work.

Why...

➤ Working hard does not guarantee results.

Look for...

➤ Obstacles created by poor job design such as poor process flow or unnecessary steps.

➤ Antiquated or inappropriate equipment or materials.

➤ Little agreement on what constitutes good work.

Do...

➤ Eliminate unnecessary steps.

➤ Provide up-to-date technology and materials.

➤ Clarify what the goals are.

➤ Provide productivity feedback.

Great resistance to change.

Why...

➤ People are not resistant to change, they resist **being** changed.

➤ People are more afraid of the unknown future than of the known present and uncertainty over what the world will look like after the change.

➤ Stakeholders are not convinced that making the change will be "worth it."

Look for...

➤ Rumors that sow seeds of doubt.

➤ Misunderstanding about the time and process for change.

➤ Opportunities for selling the change.

Do...

➤ Set up easy, direct-to-the-top communication channels.

➤ Offer evidence that failure to change has negative consequences.

➤ Widen decision-making to include as many players as possible.

➤ Leave details of the change to implementation-level players.

➤ Offer convincing evidence that post-change conditions will be exactly as predicted and worth the effort.

Customers report that service is not friendly.

Why...

➤ If the customer says that service is not friendly, it is not friendly.

Look for...

➤ Differences between customer expectations and organization standards.

➤ Micro-insults that may be influencing customer opinion.

➤ Customer service and services provided by the competition.

Do...

➤ Survey to discover exact customer expectations.

➤ Analyze how expectations are being managed.

➤ Discover and eliminate micro-insults.

➤ Train players in customer expectations and service strategies.

➤ Eliminate obstacles to friendly service such as poor hiring, poor training and short staffing.

Customers report that service is slow.

Why...

➤ Service is not a matter of speed; it is a matter of perception.

Look for...

➤ Environmental elements that may influence the perception of speed.

➤ Service provided by the competition and in other industries that may not be related that may influence the situation.

➤ Discover your customer's exact expectations of service speed.

Do...

➤ Eliminate waiting where possible.

➤ Make waiting more interesting or pleasant where possible.

➤ Make waiting a benefit by providing extra service, training, etc.

➤ If waiting is done in person, use a serpentine queue to make waiting more fair and to make the line seem to move faster.

Customers complain that orders are often filled inaccurately.

Why...

➤ Accurate order-filling is often a matter of perception.

Look for...

➤ Ways the customer contributes to the accuracy of the order.

➤ Ways that the system could be changed to put the customer in charge.

➤ Ways the system encourages error, i.e., through using arcane order-units.

Do...

➤ Verify the order before filling.

➤ Eliminate confusing descriptions of units of measure.

➤ Give customers feedback on order accuracy to manage expectations.

Customers will not buy unless "on deal."

Why...

➤ Customers, like employees, are trained in their behavior.

➤ Customers are not stupid. They recognize value when you tell them!

Look for...

➤ Instances where customers are being trained to expect a deal.

➤ Opportunities to shape customer perception of value.

➤ Opportunities to bundle, creating a perception of a bigger deal.

Do...

➤ Eliminate predictable discounting.

➤ Eliminate discounting on core products.

➤ Create bundles that offer discounts. i.e. the customer has to do something extra to get something extra.

➤ Refuse to deal on price; deal on terms and service.

➤ Take advantage of every opportunity or create opportunities to make value tangible.

High accident rate.

Why...

➤ There are no accidents, only unexpected results.

Look for...

➤ Equipment or processes that contribute to accidents.

➤ Correlations between time, place or product and accidents.

Do...

➤ Eliminate opportunities for accidents.

➤ Repair or replace equipment.

➤ Train players in procedures.

➤ Provide feedback and reinforcement for safe behavior.

High grievance rate.

Why...

➤ People never complain about themselves. It's always the other guy.

➤ When the players are in control, there is no need to complain; only a need to make things better.

Look for...

➤ Anything that fosters a "them vs. us" mentality.

➤ Are team players in control of the work environment or is everything a matter to be decreed from on high?

Do...

➤ Shut up and listen.

➤ Get out with the troops and demonstrate that you understand.

➤ Ask for help in identifying "stupid." There will be plenty to find.

➤ Create ways for operatives to contribute. Ask for, then act on suggestions for improvement. Reward great suggestions.

High turnover.

Why...

➤ Working for you is a bore.

➤ Who wants to work where it's not fun?

➤ Stress occurs at all levels. It's the number one cause of turnover.

Look for...

➤ Signs of repetitive, boring, restrictive work.

➤ Signs that people are uncertain of what is expected of them.

➤ Frequent changes or inconsistent job requirements.

➤ Customers who are aggressive, rude and/or overly demanding.

Do...

➤ Assign work to teams and let the team complete an entire process.

➤ Clarify goals.

➤ Provide lots of positive feedback.

➤ Train management to act as a team, too, to give consistent instruction.

➤ Review the order system to make certain that customers know how to order and that yelling is not necessary.

➤ Train, train, train.

Theft...of time, tools, customers and cash.

Why...

➤ People never steal from themselves. Your players have no buy-in.

➤ Some people are natural thieves.

Look for...

➤ Autocratic management style.

➤ Opportunities to rationalize theft as "getting what I deserved."

➤ Poor hiring practices that fail to screen thieves and drug abusers.

➤ Opportunities to steal without getting caught...temptation.

➤ An example set by management, such as golfing on company time.

Do...

➤ Move to a more democratic management style.

➤ Remove overt temptation temporarily.

➤ Set an example of scrupulous honesty in all dealings.

➤ Learn to screen applicants thoroughly.

➤ Eliminate any chance that employees are not fully paid and fairly treated.

Lip service given to mission but little or no action.

Why...

➤ If you don't believe it, I don't believe it.

➤ A fish rots from its head down and a dead fish smells awful for a long, long time.

Look for...

➤ Example set by management.

➤ Disincentives for actually making the change.

➤ A history of inconsistency, chasing the latest management fad.

Do...

➤ Involve the team in setting the mission.

➤ Provide positive feedback.

➤ Celebrate progress and those who contribute.

➤ Be prepared for the change to take a long time.

➤ Set the example, go first and go all the way.

➤ Be willing to lose a few key players.

➤ If you build it, they will come...eventually.

High morale, high productivity.

Why...

➤ A system left to itself will eventually run down hill.

➤ Leaving things well enough alone is a recipe for disaster in a changing world.

Look for...

➤ Early signs of deterioration.

➤ Potential for the technology or the market to mature.

➤ Changes in the market or technology that could make your product obsolete.

Do...

➤ Continue to celebrate successes.

➤ Begin to recreate yourself before being forced to do so.

➤ Introduce enough challenge to keep the system responsive.

➤ Raise the bar.

Difficulty recruiting winners.

Why...

➤ Winning team players have choices. Yours isn't the best choice.

Look for...

➤ Competing opportunities that attract your potential hire.

➤ Reasons why winners would not even apply with you.

Do...

➤ View recruiting as a marketing process — you need a message and a delivery system.

➤ Create an attractive work environment before you attempt to sell.

➤ Offer rewards, only to the winners you already have on staff, for recruiting more just like them.

➤ Survey winning team players to find out why they were attracted to their present job.

New employees start strong but performance quickly deteriorates.

Why...

➤ You're doing a good job recruiting, hiring and training.

➤ It's the management or the system that stinks.

Look for...

➤ Reasons why employees may lose their enthusiasm.

➤ Non-performing old-timers that may have a reason for holding down production, i.e., concern that standards will be raised.

Do...

➤ Ask your internal customers what they would change about the job.

➤ Create work teams responsible for entire processes.

➤ Provide frequent, positive feedback for performers.

➤ Base individual compensation in part on team performance.

Employees ignore procedures.

Why...

➤ When there are two or more competing incentives, the one that is most desirable always wins.

Look for...

➤ Ways that not following procedures are being reinforced.

➤ Possibility that procedures are not clearly understood.

Do...

➤ Clarify the procedures including the reasoning behind them.

➤ Stamp out stupid.

➤ Discover and eliminate the competing reinforcer for not following procedures or the punishment for doing things by the book.

Team members work hard...but not together.

Why...

➤ People work together when they have both permission and purpose.

Look for...

➤ Organizational quirks that may discourage teamwork.

➤ Potential disincentive for working together, particularly reinforcing individual performance.

➤ Reasons why people may not know or believe they should work together, i.e., conflicting goals or personalities.

Do...

➤ Create reinforcements for teamwork.

➤ Promote teamwork.

➤ Redesign the work process to encourage teamwork.

➤ Consider changing players or field positions.

➤ Create group goals.

Workplace cluttered with sacred cows.

Why...

➤ No one knows why sacred cows are allowed to live. They can't be shot until you find out who is the owner.

Look for...

➤ Sacred cows that have no owner. Shoot them on the spot.

➤ The history behind sacred cows.

➤ Possible benefits of allowing them to live, perhaps even fatten.

➤ Potential for training your sacred cows.

Do...

➤ Find the owners of sacred cows and ask if they are
really sacred.

➤ Play "Stamp out Stupid" and "Things we don't do, but could."

➤ Think of ways sacred cows could be put to good use.

➤ Think of ways sacred cows could be replaced by sacred bulls.

2

MANAGER'S TOOLBOX

MISSION STATEMENT CRITERIA

Short...easy to remember.

In your face...always top of mind.

Incorporates founding principles.

May incorporate key strategy.

Mentions the product and the targeted customer.

Mentions the uniqueness of the organization.

Three simple steps to changing an organization:

Change one person at a time.

Be patient until you build "critical mass."

Change yourself first.

Getting Ready for Change

Present...where are you right now?

_____

_____

Future...what do you want to be when you grow up?

_____

_____

247

On what basis did you make the above decision?

_____

_____

Dreaming the dream

Who gets to help build the dream? Customers? Suppliers? Internal customers?

_____

How do we get from where we are to where we want to be? What financial resources may be required? Can we make that kind of commitment? Are the funds available?

_____

_____

What human resources will be required? Do we have them? Can we get them?

_____

_____

What sacrifices will be required? Are we willing to make the sacrifices, including losing current team players?

_____

_____

How do we sell the dream?

_____

_____

What Workers Want

(From _American Demographics_, August, 1992)

____ Good health insurance and other benefits

____ Interesting work

____ Job security

____ Opportunity to learn new job skills

____ Annual vacations of week or more

____ Freedom to work independently

____ Recognition from co-workers

____ Having a job in which you can help others

____ Limited job stress

____ Regular hours, no nights or weekends

____ High income
____ Working close to home
____ Work that is important to society
____ Chances for promotion
____ Contact with a lot of people

Service is an intangible product created for an individual customer at the point of sale.

ORGANIZATIONAL CHANGE PROCESS STEPS

Determine baseline.

Find out what you already know...or could easily know.

Determine objectives.

    Reward performance.

    Discover opportunities to improve performance.

    Discover opportunities to improve the system.

Create the survey system.

Choose measures that target the objectives.

    Are the measures actionable?

    Choose measurement media.

    Who will be surveyed?

Create the instrument or vehicle.

    Ask customers to make "trade-offs."

Encourage response.

Test for "what ifs" that could shape results.

Put the system to test, then to work.

Use rank and score to survey.

    Determine weights.

    Watch for minimum expectations. (Don't confuse eliminators with determinants.)

Analyze data.

    Would a composite measure be valuable?

Evaluate the process.

Provide training.

    Pro-active.

    Remedial.

Post results.

Provide feedback to participants.

SCOTT'S LAW OF EXPANSION:
A business will expand to accommodate the number
of winning team players it hires.
Hire all the winners. Get all the business.

Hiring a team of winners? Follow these steps:

➤ Define what the customer thinks is a winner...develop a profile.
➤ Survey and improve your offer where possible.
➤ Audition to the profile.
➤ Create an individual training plan and get started.
➤ Survey to discover right up front what motivates your candidates individually.
➤ Create a performance contract to set standards of performance for both parties.
➤ Occasionally test your hiring decision against customer feedback.
➤ Occasionally test your training and incentive program against team player feedback.

THE MOST EFFECTIVE FEEDBACK IS....

Immediate
Positive
Specific
Personalized
Self-monitored
Related to baseline performance
Easily understood
Sincere

FOR MORE EFFECTIVE DELIVERY OF REINFORCEMENT...

➤ Make certain that the reinforcement is perceived as such.
➤ Make it personal.
➤ Reinforce immediately.
➤ Reinforce frequently.
➤ Make the reinforcement behavior specific.
➤ Never use the "sandwich" method.
➤ Never reinforce and punish at the same time.

CONTESTS THAT WORK...

➤ Have specific goals.

➤ Are self-liquidating.

➤ Are simple, easy to understand.

➤ Require promotion.

➤ Must not be repeats of previous contests.

➤ Are preceded by training with every contest — good contests are learning experiences.

➤ Have visible rewards throughout the contest.

➤ Make it possible for everyone to win.

➤ Keep the term appropriate for the group.

➤ Make certain that the reward is "worth it".

➤ Have participants competing against their individual performance or a common standard.

➤ Have players keep their own score.

➤ Offer latitude in the participant's choosing the reward.

➤ Work best when short-term behaviors are desired.

➤ Level the playing field.

➤ Give feedback frequently, if not constantly.

OUR LIST OF TEAM BUILDING TACTICS...

Celebrate and reward team performance.

Organize work around team performance.

Organize the physical plant to encourage teamwork.

Create a goal impossible to reach without teamwork.

Create communications systems that foster teamwork.

GREAT TEAM LEADERS...

Are good followers

Have specialized skills needed by the team

Are excellent communicators

Are capable facilitators

Field team players to best advantage

Turn goals into objectives

Make progress tangible

Serve as team champion

THREE INVALUABLE LESSONS:

➤ You can do more with less when you really believe that you have to.

➤ Faced with the choice of studying a problem or taking your best shot...shoot.

➤ If you want people to pay for your ideas, you must first sell them.

HOW TO ENCOURAGE TEAMPLAY:

➤ Let the team know that they are a team.

➤ Get on the team yourself.

➤ Step on gossip...hard.

➤ Create a crisis or other challenge.

➤ Reward cooperation vs. competition.

TEAM PLAYER'S BILL OF RIGHTS

I have the right to...

➤ Know how I am doing.

➤ Be properly trained for the task at hand.

➤ Earn the right for reduced supervision.

➤ Work in a safe, non-threatening environment.

➤ Have a share in the fruits of my labor.

➤ Be listened to whether my ideas are brilliant or not.

➤ Be respected as a human being.

➤ Expect honest, open communications.

➤ Know how the organization is faring.

➤ Make decisions without fear so long as they are made with integrity.

MasterMedia Limited
17 East 89th Street
New York, NY 10128
(212) 260-5600
(800) 334-8232 *please use Mastercard or Visa on 1-800 orders*
(212) 546-7638 (fax)

OTHER MASTERMEDIA BUSINESS BOOKS

POSITIVELY OUTRAGEOUS SERVICE: New and Easy Ways to Win Customers for Life, by T. Scott Gross, identifies what the consumers of the nineties really want and how businesses can develop effective marketing strategies to answer those needs. ($14.95 paper)

POSITIVELY OUTRAGEOUS SERVICE AND SHOWMANSHIP: Industrial Strength Fun Makes Sales Sizzle!!!!, by T. Scott Gross, reveals the secrets of adding personality to any product or service. ($12.95 paper)

HOW TO GET WHAT YOU WANT FROM ALMOST ANYBODY, by T. Scott Gross, shows how to get great service, negotiate better prices, and always get what you pay for. ($9.95 paper)

OUT THE ORGANIZATION: New Career Opportunities for the 1990's, by Robert and Madeleine Swain, is written for the millions of Americans whose jobs are no longer safe, whose companies are not loyal, and who face futures of uncertainty. It gives advice on finding a new job or starting your own business. ($12.95 paper)

CRITICISM IN YOUR LIFE: How to Give It, How to Take It, How to Make It Work for You, by Dr. Deborah Bright, offers practical advice, in an upbeat, readable, and realistic fashion, for turning criticism into control. Charts and diagrams guide the reader into managing criticism from bosses, spouses, children, friends, neighbors, in-laws, and business relations. ($17.95 cloth)

BEYOND SUCCESS: How Volunteer Service Can Help You Begin Making a Life Instead of Just a Living, by John F. Raynolds III and Eleanor Raynolds, C.B.E., is a unique how-to book targeted at business and professional people considering volunteer work, senior citizens who wish to fill leisure time meaningfully, and students trying out various career options. The book is filled with interviews with celebrities, CEOs, and average citizens who talk about the benefits of service work. ($19.95 cloth)

MANAGING IT ALL: Time-Saving Ideas for Career, Family, Relationships, and Self, by Beverly Benz Treuille and Susan Schiffer Stautberg, is written for women who are juggling careers and families. Over two hundred career women (ranging from a TV anchorwoman to an investment banker) were interviewed. The book contains many humorous anecdotes on saving time and improving the quality of life for self and family. ($9.95 paper)

THE CONFIDENCE FACTOR: How Self-Esteem Can Change Your Life, by Dr. Judith Briles, is based on a nationwide survey of six thousand men and women. Briles explores why women so often feel a lack of self-confidence and have a poor opinion of themselves. She offers step-by-step advice on becoming the person you want to be. ($9.95 paper, $18.95 cloth)

TAKING CONTROL OF YOUR LIFE: The Secrets of Successful Enterprising Women, by Gail Blanke and Kathleen Walas, is based on the authors' professional experience with Avon Products' Women of Enterprise Awards, given each year to outstanding women entrepreneurs. The authors offer a specific plan to help you gain control over your life, and include business tips and quizzes as well as beauty and lifestyle information. ($17.95 cloth)

SIDE-BY-SIDE STRATEGIES: How Two-Career Couples Can Thrive in the Nineties, by Jane Hershey Cuozzo and S. Diane Graham, describes how two-career couples can learn the difference between competing with a spouse and becoming a supportive power partner. Published in hardcover as *Power Partners.* ($10.95 paper, $19.95 cloth)

WORK WITH ME! How to Make the Most of Office Support Staff, by Betsy Lazary, shows you how to find, train, and nurture the "perfect" assistant and how to best utilize your support staff professionals. ($9.95 paper)

THE LOYALTY FACTOR: Building Trust in Today's Workplace, by Carol Kinsey Goman, Ph.D., offers techniques for restoring commitment and loyalty in the workplace. ($9.95 paper)

DARE TO CHANGE YOUR JOB—AND YOUR LIFE, by Carole Kanchier, Ph.D., provides a look at career growth and development throughout the life cycle. ($9.95 paper)

BREATHING SPACE: Living and Working at a Comfortable Pace in a Sped-Up Society, by Jeff Davidson, helps readers to handle information and activity overload, and gain greater control over their lives. ($10.95 paper)

TWENTYSOMETHING: Managing and Motivating Today's New Work Force, by Lawrence J. Bradford, Ph.D., and Claire Raines, M.A., examines the work orientation of the younger generation, offering managers in businesses of all kinds a practical guide to better understand and supervise their young employees. ($22.95 cloth)

BALANCING ACTS! Juggling Love, Work, Family, and Recreation, by Susan Schiffer Stautberg and Marcia L. Worthing, provides strategies to achieve a balanced life by reordering priorities and setting realistic goals. ($12.95 paper)

STEP FORWARD: Sexual Harassment in the Workplace, What You Need to Know, by Susan L. Webb, presents the facts for identifying the tell-tale signs of sexual harassment on the job, and how to deal with it. ($9.95 paper)

A TEEN'S GUIDE TO BUSINESS: The Secrets to a Successful Enterprise, by Linda Menzies, Oren S. Jenkins, and Rickell R. Fisher, provides solid information about starting your own business or working for one. ($7.95 paper)

TEAMBUILT: Making Teamwork Work, by Mark Sanborn, teaches business how to improve productivity, without increasing resources or expenses, by building teamwork among employers. ($19.95 cloth)